Samuel French Acting Edition

A Home for Stray Cats
A Mystery in Three Acts

by John Kirkpatrick

Copyright © 1969 by John Kirkpatrick
All Rights Reserved

A HOME FOR STRAY CATS is fully protected under the copyright laws of the United States of America, the British Commonwealth, including Canada, and all other countries of the Copyright Union. All rights, including professional and amateur stage productions, recitation, lecturing, public reading, motion picture, radio broadcasting, television and the rights of translation into foreign languages are strictly reserved.

ISBN 978-0-573-61021-9

www.SamuelFrench.com
www.SamuelFrench.co.uk

FOR PRODUCTION ENQUIRIES

UNITED STATES AND CANADA
Info@SamuelFrench.com
1-866-598-8449

UNITED KINGDOM AND EUROPE
Plays@SamuelFrench.co.uk
020-7255-4302

Each title is subject to availability from Samuel French, depending upon country of performance. Please be aware that *A HOME FOR STRAY CATS* may not be licensed by Samuel French in your territory. Professional and amateur producers should contact the nearest Samuel French office or licensing partner to verify availability.

CAUTION: Professional and amateur producers are hereby warned that *A HOME FOR STRAY CATS* is subject to a licensing fee. Publication of this play(s) does not imply availability for performance. Both amateurs and professionals considering a production are strongly advised to apply to Samuel French before starting rehearsals, advertising, or booking a theatre. A licensing fee must be paid whether the title(s) is presented for charity or gain and whether or not admission is charged. Professional/Stock licensing fees are quoted upon application to Samuel French.

No one shall make any changes in this title(s) for the purpose of production. No part of this book may be reproduced, stored in a retrieval system, or transmitted in any form, by any means, now known or yet to be invented, including mechanical, electronic, photocopying, recording, videotaping, or otherwise, without the prior written permission of the publisher. No one shall upload this title(s), or part of this title(s), to any social media websites.

For all enquiries regarding motion picture, television, and other media rights, please contact Samuel French.

Please refer to page 97 for further copyright information.

STORY OF THE PLAY

From the time Louise Vickers arrives at the shadowy old country house, she notices a change in her secretary. Harriet is rude and antagonistic to all the people in the house, particularly to Elizabeth Byron, the owner. Louise discovers that Harriet was once engaged to Tom Byron, Elizabeth's alcoholic brother. Harriet is stabbed to death and the rich elderly invalid upstairs dies of fright. Was there something else in Harriet's past life, or had she stumbled on some secret involving the prospective heirs of the invalid? Why was Martha pretending to be a servant when she obviously wasn't? Why did the young musician drug the trained nurse? And what of Corinne, recently recovered from a nervous breakdown, who now walks in her sleep? And wasn't Mrs. Smythe, the sweet and gentle bore, just a little too good to be true? Tensely and with great skill, the author unfolds this psychological thriller and arrives at a starling denouement.

CHARACTERS
(In the Order in Which They Speak)

MRS. SMYTHE

LOUISE VICKERS

HARRIET BEAM

ELIZABETH BYRON

NURSE (MISS GREEN)

MARTHA

CORINNE WALKER

RONNIE BLISS

TOM BYRON

LIEUTENANT SCOTT, *of the Connecticut State Police*

ELKINS, *also of the Police*

The action of the play takes place at "Linden Lodge," in the countryside of Connecticut.

The time is an evening in spring.

During Act Two the curtain will be lowered to denote the passing of fifteen minutes.

A Home for Stray Cats

ACT ONE

SCENE: *If we could see the outside of the house, we would find it one of those country "mansions," built around 1910—the ugly period of American architecture—a house with turrets, cupolas, bay windows, stained glass, a porte cochere and much grillwork and doodads. The scene is of an odd shape and set obliquely. It represents two distinct rooms thrown together. The living area is Down Right and extends towards the Left; the dining area is Up Left and slightly resembles an alcove. Beginning at the proscenium arch, Right, and moving Upstage, there is a fireplace, and then a French window. In the Upstage wall of the living area is a wide arch, opening into the hall. The front door of the house is out of sight at Right. The Upstage wall of the living area joins the Right wall of the dining area at a ninety-degree angle. In this wall of the dining area is another, but smaller arch, which, of course, also opens into the hall. In the Upstage wall of the dining area is a swinging door, leading into pantry, kitchen, etc. The Left wall of the dining area is a rounded wall with high-up casement window, underneath which is a built-in sideboard. In the angle where the Upstage wall of the living room joins the Right wall of the dining room, there is a table, with a telephone on it. The table and telephone, of course, are not seen, but a person using the phone can step away from the table and may be seen through either the large arch or the small arch. In the living room are several comfortable chairs, coffeetable, etc. The chairs towards the Left*

*should be low-backed, so as not to obstruct the view
of the action in the dining area. In the dining area
is a table, with five chairs around it. The hall is never
very brightly lighted, but way Upstage may be dimly
seen the suggestion of a newel post and stairs leading
up; also the beginning of a passage leading to the
back of the house. These can be only dimly viewed,
and can't be seen at all from certain sections of the
auditorium. This does not matter as no important
action takes place there; but we know they are there,
from the dialogue and the business. IMPORTANT
NOTE: Characters, leaving the dining area for the
living area, sometimes move Downstage and cross towards Right; at other times, when* expressly called
for in the direction, *they exit by small arch (the arch
in the dining room) pass out of sight for a few seconds, and then reappear at wide arch (the arch in
living room).*

AT RISE: *Three women are finishing dinner.* ELIZABETH
BYRON *is thirty-two but seems older. She would probably be a handsome woman if she were "fixed up"
with the proper hair-do, clothes, make-up. Lacking
these things, she appears a bit gaunt, almost grim.
She is slim and tall. One sees in her a woman who
has had just a bit too much to cope with; she is
under control, but one wonders how long the control
will last.* HARRIET BEAM *is dark, in the middle
twenties. Her good looks are marred by eyes which
are too cold, too brutal, and by a mouth which curves
down to give her an unpleasant sullen look. An un-
happy woman, whose unhappiness comes not from
encounter with the world about her, but from within.
A vague restlessness, groping to release itself and,
until it does, self-centered and intolerant. The other
woman,* BLOSSOM SMYTHE, *is fortyish, sweet, coy, a
chatter-box who goes on and on, utterly tactless and
a horrible bore.*

ACT I A HOME FOR STRAY CATS 7

MRS. SMYTHE. Such a lovely book! I started reading it today to dear Mrs. Gensett. And every now and then I just had to stop and say, "Isn't it *lovely*, Mrs. Gensett?" And she'd say "Lovely!" There's the most *beautiful* description of Venice! The church, San Marco—that's St. Marks, you know. . . .

(*The others are not listening;* BOTH *seem to be straining to hear something else; and even* MRS. SMYTHE *pauses every now and then to hear it. The something else is a woman's voice—that of* LOUISE VICKERS— *speaking on a telephone in the hall. We hear it clearly.*)

LOUISE. (*Offstage.*) Yes. . . . Two of us—but *three* rooms. That's quite important. I want a sitting room. Yes. . . . I'll wait!

MRS. SMYTHE. . . . and the pigeons on the piazza— Italian for "square," you know and . . . oh, that thing that goes across the . . . the Ponte dei Sospiri. That's the—

HARRIET. (*Bitingly.*) Bridge of Sighs. We know.

MRS. SMYTHE. (*Delightedly.*) Oh, do you speak Italian, Miss—er—?

HARRIET. (*Shortly.*) No. And the name is "Beam." "Beam." I've told you three times.

MRS. SMYTHE. (*Laughing, and completely undismayed.*) I know. I know you have. But I'm so stupid about names.

HARRIET. Is that the only thing that you're—that bothers you?

MRS. SMYTHE. Oh, I have a marvelous memory for everything else. You know I can read a book—and tell people everything that's in it.

HARRIET. Yes, we know.

MRS. SMYTHE. (*Laughing.*) My dear husband—such a *good* man!—used to say to me—that is, when he was alive—he used to say, "Blossom, how in the world can you remember so much of—?"

HARRIET. Is that *really* your name? "Blossom"?
MRS. SMYTHE. (*That laugh again.*) Silly, isn't it? But I was born in the springtime. My father just adored nature. Sometimes I think he loved nature more than . . . Well, every chance he got, he'd be out of the house. He was the— (*She stops; and listens.*)
LOUISE. (*On phone.*) Oh? I see. The name is Vickers. Mrs. Louise Vickers. And we . . . Wait, please. I wonder if I may call you about this in the morning? . . . What? No . . . No. . . . I'll call you . . . In the morning. And . . . thank you. In the morning. And—thank you.

(HARRIET *frowns.* ELIZABETH *seems slightly relieved.*)

MRS. SMYTHE. Isn't it funny the way you listen to somebody on a telephone? You try not to listen, of course, but— Where was I? (*She turns to* ELIZABETH.) Where was I?
ELIZABETH. Oh, I—I'm sorry, Mrs. Smythe. I—I don't believe I— I'm sorry.

(LOUISE VICKERS *appears at arch to living room, and stands there.* LOUISE *is fifty-five, a small woman with a kind, intelligent face and a slim, trim figure. Her speech is crisp, incisive; her movements graceful, but determined.*)

MRS. SMYTHE. Venice! That's where— Imagine forgetting Venice! Antonia—that's the girl's name—lived in Venice. Italian, you know. I think "Antonia's" such a lovely name for a girl, don't you? I mean—for an Italian girl?

(*She looks from one to the other of the* TWO WOMEN *at the table. But their thoughts are elsewhere. Her eyes narrow, and for the first time we wonder if she is quite such a fool as she pretends.* LOUISE *comes into living room.*)

ACT I A HOME FOR STRAY CATS 9

LOUISE. (*Raising her voice a little.*) Miss Byron, I wonder if I might speak to you just a moment.

ELIZABETH. Excuse me. (*She rises, comes Downstage, and towards Right.* LOUISE *has moved towards fireplace.*)

MRS. SMYTHE. Of course she and Lord Claypool had met before. In London. He was—

HARRIET. Not English! Don't tell me he was English! I couldn't bear it!

MRS. SMYTHE. Why, yes. But how in the world did you—?

(HARRIET *rises abruptly, tosses her napkin on the table and follows* ELIZABETH *to the other room. Again that odd expression on* MRS. SMYTHE'S *face.*)

LOUISE. I wonder if it would be convenient for us to stay on—for a few days anyway.

HARRIET. (*Before the* OTHER *can answer.*) Why? They had rooms there, didn't they?

LOUISE. Yes, but I don't feel quite equal to making the move just now.

HARRIET. Much better to get settled. And since you don't like it here—

LOUISE. Harriet! (*She looks at* ELIZABETH.)

HARRIET. What? Oh. You know what I mean. No place to work—

LOUISE. I'll manage somehow. My bedroom or—

HARRIET. You loathe working in your bedroom. You always did.

LOUISE. Yes, but—packing—moving—

HARRIET. We're not *un*packed. Not really.

LOUISE. No. I've changed my mind. I shall stay here.

HARRIET. Hm. I don't think you intended to move in the first place.

LOUISE. (*Smiles at* ELIZABETH.) Perhaps I didn't. Perhaps I really wanted to stay in your very lovely home, Miss—

HARRIET. Not "lovely"! Dear God! Not that! That

woman in there's used that word eighteen times in— (*She checks her nerves and finishes, ungraciously.*) Well, suit yourself. (*She takes a step as if to go. Then:*) Could I have my coffee in here instead of on the Grand Canal?

ELIZABETH. Of course. I'm very glad you're staying, Mrs. Vickers. When my brother gets back, I'm sure we can work out something. I know you don't like writing in your bedroom, so—

LOUISE. Well, I dictate a lot—pace up and down—kicking at the furniture—

ELIZABETH. (*Smiles.*) Yes. Miss Beam told me. I was going to turn that big corner room over to you. I suppose when my aunt arrived, I should have called you up—told you not to come—

HARRIET. Why didn't you?

LOUISE. Harriet!

ELIZABETH. Quite frankly, Miss Beam, I needed the money.

LOUISE. That's a motive we can all understand these days. I'm afraid I've been difficult. All the fuss I've made over an extra room. Under ordinary circumstances, I assure you, I should have taken it in my stride. It's just that—I haven't been feeling up to scratch lately. . . . Not sleeping properly—

ELIZABETH. When the doctor comes to see my aunt, would you like him to give you some sleeping tablets or—

LOUISE. I have some, thank you. I suppose it's really a guilt complex. I'm behind on my new book—

HARRIET. "Behind"? You haven't even started it!

LOUISE. (*Looks at her.*) No.

HARRIET. Ha! You haven't even got an idea, have you?

LOUISE. (*Another quick look.*) No. But I can't believe Miss Byron is interested in—

HARRIET. You started it!

LOUISE. Then perhaps you'll let me finish it.

(*The starched white figure of a* NURSE *appears briefly at the LIVING ROOM arch.*)

NURSE. That maid—or whatever she calls herself—didn't show up. I had to bring the trays down myself. (*She disappears towards back of hall.*)

ELIZABETH. I'm sorry. Thank you, Miss Green.

LOUISE. We'll try not to make any extra work for you. An invalid—especially an elderly invalid—a nurse—special diets—must present quite a problem.

HARRIET. Tell me, Miss Byron. Does your aunt often descend upon you in this way? (LOUISE *starts to speak. She is not only shocked at* HARRIET'S *manner, but strangely puzzled by it.* HARRIET *has seen* LOUISE'S *look, and shrugs.*) Just curiosity. She doesn't have to answer.

ELIZABETH. (*With an odd smile.*) No, I don't, do I? But I will. My aunt, Miss Beam, has been "descending," as you call it—on me—and various other members of the family—for the last five years. Ever since she broke up her own home. She dislikes hotels—

LOUISE. I do myself.

ELIZABETH. Without the slightest warning—or a by-your-leave—without in the least considering whether it's convenient or not—she just "descends." Furthermore—

LOUISE. You don't have to explain, you know.

ELIZABETH. I think I'd better. When I have, perhaps you won't want to stay even a few days. Or—Miss Beam won't. (*To* HARRIET.) Furthermore, after she's been in a place for a while—completely disrupted the household—set everybody by the ears—she gets in a rage—moves on to somewhere else—and starts the process all over again.

LOUISE. You poor dear. I always thought Dante should have shown us what happens to visiting relatives.

HARRIET. You must all love her very much—or else—she must be extremely rich.

LOUISE. Really, Harriet! That's just a bit too—

ELIZABETH. (*To* HARRIET.) I'll answer that too, Miss Beam. My aunt is extremely rich—and the rest of us are extremely—poor. Is there anything else you'd like to know?

LOUISE. (*Quietly.*) No, Miss Byron. There's nothing

else. In spite of what you've told us, I still think we'll stay. At least, *I* will. My—secretary may do as she chooses.

(ELIZABETH *nods towards* LOUISE, *and goes out arch to back of hall.*)

HARRIET. So I'm being put in my place.
LOUISE. You deserve every bit of it. What *is* the matter with you? Why are you so—rude—to Miss Byron—everyone? What is it? (HARRIET *lowers her eyes and a stubborn, sullen look comes into her face.*) I—wish you'd tell me, because I'm—just a little tired of apologizing for you.
HARRIET. Would you like to fire me?
LOUISE. Would you like me to?
HARRIET. If my work isn't satisfactory—
LOUISE. You *know* that it is. This is—grotesque. You and I talking like this. After our . . . We were fond of each other. At least I thought so. And now—something must have happened. I've—never interfered with your personal life—
HARRIET. Then don't start now!
LOUISE. I don't intend to—except in so far as it concerns me. In town you come to the apartment for so many hours—and that's that. But when we go away together, we stay at the same place—are thrown with the same people—the conduct of one of us is obliged to reflect on the other. Your sudden lack of manners—decent ordinary *manners* is—

(*She stops, as the maid,* MARTHA, *comes through living room arch, with coffee tray.* MARTHA *is quite pretty, but the maid's outfit is just a shade too large for her. And she is obviously untrained in her job. It's not that she is personally awkward; she just doesn't know, gets rattled and does the wrong thing. As she serves the coffee, there are a few moments of silence.* LOUISE *has extracted from her bag a small notebook, with pencil attached, and is making notes. In the dining room,* Mrs. Smythe *is reading her book.*)

Harriet. Do you have to slosh the coffee over into the saucer?
Martha. I'll get another cup.
Harriet. Never mind.
Nurse. (*She comes through swinging door, and speaks to* Mrs. Smythe.) I'd be glad if you didn't read to my patient so long. It tires her.
Mrs. Smythe. But, nurse, Mrs. Gensett *likes* me to read to her. And this new book we've started—
Nurse. Not over an hour, please. (*She goes to dining room arch into hall.* Mrs. Smythe *looks after her venomously.* Martha *has moved to offer sugar to* Louise, *as the* Nurse *appears at Living Room arch.*) Martha! (Martha *pays no attention.*)
Louise. I think she's speaking to you.

(Martha *wheels around.* Louise *wonders at this.*)

Nurse. Your name is "Martha," isn't it?
Martha. Yes.
Nurse. Weren't you taught to say "miss"—or "ma'am" or something? (Martha *doesn't answer.*) You didn't bring my coffee. I'll have it now upstairs.
Martha. I—I don't think there is any more. And the cook's gone to bed.
Nurse. Then make some yourself!

(*She moves Upstage into back to stairs.* Martha *slams the sugar bowl on tray, and she goes towards back of hall.*)

Harriet. You'll never get anything done in this place. And without even an *idea*—
Louise. Twice you've said that. I'll get an idea—
Harriet. Hope it's better than the last one. (*It's doubt-*

ful if she really meant to say this; but now that she has.) All right. I said it. Your last book was pretty much of a flop, you know. And it's no good quoting the sales. You skidded along on your reputation—but you did skid. Too tame. Books these days have to have a punch—a wallop—a knockout. That kind of thing! Bang—crash—boom!

LOUISE. Whew! You make writing sound a little like the charge up San Juan Hill.

HARRIET. Well, it is, isn't it? *Your* kind of writing.

LOUISE. I—I like to think there's a little bit more involved.

HARRIET. Oh, technique—all that stuff. But in a mystery story, what counts is the end—the gimmick—the twist—the sock! The world moves, you know.

LOUISE. Yes, I know. But I'm still riding on it.

HARRIET. One gentle murder isn't enough these days. You have to keep on killing people—right and left—until— (*She happens to glance towards arch;* ELIZABETH *is standing there with a cup of coffee in her hand.*) You want something?

ELIZABETH. I? No. (*To* LOUISE.) Except I'm making more coffee. If you—or Miss Beam—would— (LOUISE *smiles, shakes her head.* ELIZABETH *leaves arch, and appears at other arch, to Dining Room. She goes to table.*) I'm late with this. The maid is new—she forgets. (*She leans over to put the cup in front of* MRS. SMYTHE.)

MRS. SMYTHE. Quite all right. I was just reading away. Ha! Ha! Just reading away!

A WOMAN'S VOICE. (*From Hallway.*) Elizabeth!

(*At the sound of the voice,* MRS. SMYTHE *cringes. It's almost as if she would like to crawl under the table.* ELIZABETH *turns and happens to block* MRS. SMYTHE *from the view of the woman, who appears at the small archway.* CORINNE *is forty, a plump little woman whose clothes are somewhat dowdy, a fatuous creature devoid of humor, and with a single-track mind that borders on mania.*)

ELIZABETH. I thought you'd gone.
CORINNE. Really, Elizabeth—do you think lamb chops and macaroni au gratin are the right sort of thing to serve an invalid?
ELIZABETH. It's what the "invalid" wanted. Demanded, in fact.
CORINNE. Yes, but they don't always know what's— Now when she was at *my* house—
ELIZABETH. (*Sweetly.*) But she isn't at *your* house. She left. Remember? Now she's at *my* house.
CORINNE. (*Pouting.*) You needn't talk that way. It wasn't my fault. Something Fred said to her. It—
ELIZABETH. *Please.* Corinne! I have some guests staying here.

(*She nods towards Right.* CORINNE *leaves Left arch, and in a few seconds appears at arch to living room.* ELIZABETH *goes out through swinging door.* MRS. SMYTHE *seems to breathe again, and goes ahead with her reading.*)

CORINNE. (*Coming into living room.*) How do you do? I'm Mrs. Walker. Miss Byron's cousin.
LOUISE. (*Inclines her head.*) I'm Mrs. Vickers. And this is Miss Beam. (HARRIET *hardly acknowledges the introduction.*)
CORINNE. The reason I'm staring so— Vickers. Louise Vickers! Of course. I've seen your picture on those—flap-papers—on books.
LOUISE. "Jackets." I don't know why—but they're jackets.
CORINNE. You write those awful murder things, don't you?
LOUISE. Well, I like "things." Quite apt. But just how awful did you find them?
CORINNE. Oh, I didn't mean—but you know. Blood— and gore—and goo—
LOUISE. Goo?
CORINNE. They make me shiver.

LOUISE. That was the idea.

CORINNE. My husband loves them, though. "Escape," he calls it. Though goodness only knows what he wants to escape from.

LOUISE. (*Eloquently.*) Well!

CORINNE. The other night he was reading one—one of yours, too—till two o'clock.

LOUISE. He sounds nice. I hope I meet him.

CORINNE. I tried to read it but—I hope you don't mind my saying so—it put me to sleep.

LOUISE. Part of the treatment. "Shiver and Snooze," we call it.

CORINNE. Wait till I tell Fred I've met you. Oh, and you, too, Miss Bean. Are you an author too?

HARRIET. Beam. With an M. Not that it matters. I'm her secretary. (LOUISE *gives her a quick look.*)

CORINNE. Oh. I see. You put it all down on the typewriter—and separate the colons from the semi-colons. It must be very exciting.

HARRIET. Too. You've no idea. (*Another sharp glance from* LOUISE.)

CORINNE. (*Turning to* LOUISE.) And you're staying here? I do hope you like it.

LOUISE. What makes you think we won't?

CORINNE. What? Oh, it isn't that. I'm sure Elizabeth does the best she can—under the circumstances. Tell me— have you met—her brother?

LOUISE. I liked him very much.

CORINNE. (*Eyebrows.*) Oh? But don't you find it very desolate way out here—nothing to do?

LOUISE. I've plenty to do. And I like the country. I think better.

CORINNE. Think? I thought you were a writer. It may be all right for you out here, but you must see it isn't good for Aunt Laura. I don't know if you've met Aunt Laura?

(MRS. SMYTHE *in Dining Room stops reading and is listening intently.*)

LOUISE. The invalid upstairs? No.

CORINNE. (*She is getting quite upset.*) I came to get her to come back. She was with us, but—oh, some little thing—she and Fred—just some trifle. I'm sure I could iron it out if . . . You will help me, won't you?

LOUISE. *I*, Mrs. Walker!

CORINNE. (*There is almost a wild light in her eyes.*) Yes. This place—a boarding house—you must see it's not right for her. And the doctor hates coming way out here. She should be in Bridgeport—with me. I'm sure I can get her to see that if . . . if you'll just talk to Elizabeth. Persuade her to let Aunt Laura go.

HARRIET. (*Wheels around.*) Let her go? You mean Eliz— Miss Byron *wants* her here?

CORINNE. Well, she may not *want* her—but she likes to have her around—so she and that brother of hers can work on her to get the money. Elizabeth's very sneaky— you may not know it, but—

LOUISE. Please, Mrs. Walker—

CORINNE. She is! Underhanded. But if you'd talk to her. I have four children, you know, and—

LOUISE. You have—

CORINNE. (*She's beginning to lose control.*) You don't know what it is to try and bring up four children when you don't have enough to do it on. The others don't have anybody but themselves. I keep them out of the way though. I know Aunt Laura doesn't like them, so I'm very careful. And if you'd just speak to Elizabeth about—

LOUISE. Really, Mrs. Walker, I have nothing to do with the matter.

CORINNE. But you *have*. Don't you see? You came out here to write, didn't you? Write—and think—and all that! You want it quiet. But it isn't very quiet with Aunt Laura around. Wait till she's better and can come downstairs! Bossing—and criticizing—changing everything! You won't like it here then. There won't be any quiet then. Just confusion—turmoil!

LOUISE. But you—want the turmoil! At least you—

CORINNE. No, no. I don't want it! But I have four children. . . . Please, Mrs. Vickers. It would be so easy. All you'd have to do is tell Elizabeth you couldn't stay— I mean if Aunt Laura does. Elizabeth would get the cash and—and— (*Something in* LOUISE's *face arrests her. She finishes on a different note.*) I—I don't know how Fred could do this to me. I try so—hard—and I— (*Her pudgy little face crumples up and she sinks into a chair.*)

HARRIET. (*Walks a little towards her, stops, and looks down at her with profound contempt.*) Hm. Well—

LOUISE. (*Her voice like a whiplash.*) Let her alone! Don't say a word to her!

(HARRIET *holds it a second; then stalks out through Right arch to hall, and stairs. There is a pause.*)

CORINNE. (*Without looking up.*) You—think I'm horrible.

LOUISE. No. I think that you're a very desperate woman. And I'm sorry for you. You must see that what you ask is quite impossible. But since you've asked me—perhaps you won't mind a little advice. Getting people to give you money is a fine art. And somehow I don't think you have just the qualifications for—well, the finesse. Perhaps someone else could—er—what about your husband?

CORINNE. He hates Aunt Laura. He says he'd like to kill her.

LOUISE. Why doesn't he?

CORINNE. Because we don't know how she's left her money. I mean— (*Then suddenly.*) Oh, you were joking. You don't think Fred would really k-kill anybody?

LOUISE. I don't know. I haven't met him. Tell us—this aunt of yours—Mrs. Gensett, is it?—What's wrong with her?

CORINNE. Her heart. She gets these spells—thinks she's going to die—

LOUISE. I know. I get them myself.

CORINNE. But she never does. She comes back stronger

and meaner than ever. Oh! Was that the doorbell? (*She rises.*) You never know in this house if— I suppose I'd better answer it.

(*She goes through archway into hall, and turns Right. At the sound of the BELL, Mrs. Smythe has risen and gone to dining room arch to listen. Elizabeth comes quietly through swinging door, on way to front door, but stops at seeing Mrs. Smythe.*)

Elizabeth. Expecting someone? (Mrs. Smythe, *startled, all but screams.*)

Mrs. Smythe. I was just wondering if I should—but Mrs. Walker has gone. (*Rather guiltily, she glides back to her chair and book. Elizabeth regards her curiously.*)

Corinne. (*Off Right.*) Well, really, Ronnie! This time of night!

Ronnie. (*Off Right.*) Corinne! As I live and breathe! And how are the four, dear children! (*He steps within view of archway—a personable young man of 23. He is removing his topcoat.*)

Corinne. What are you doing here?

Ronnie. To see my grrrande arrrnt Laura.

Corinne. (*She and Ronnie are still in archway.*) What do you want to see her about?

Ronnie. Wouldn't you like to know? (*He squeezes her chin.*)

Corinne. Stop that! How'd you know she was here? Elizabeth tell you?

Elizabeth. (*Still in dining room, raises her voice.*) Elizabeth did not! Hello, Ronnie.

Ronnie. (*Waving at her.*) Hiya, Liz!

(Elizabeth *exits through swinging door.*)

Corinne. (*In alarm. That wildness is beginning to return.*) She didn't send for you? Aunt Laura didn't send for you?

Ronnie. Alas, no! Alas and alack! She—

CORINNE. Then how'd you know she was here? Answer me! How'd you know she—?
RONNIE. A bird! A bird! A *bird!* Birds sit on telephone wires—pick up chit-chat. They tell other birds and— Hello. You're Mrs. Louise Vickers, aren't you? I'm Ronnie Bliss. I heard you were here. (*He gives her his most engaging smile.*)
LOUISE. The birds?

(CORINNE *has followed him into Living Room.*)

RONNIE. The birds. Would you mind awfully if I sort of—shook you by the hand?
LOUISE. (*Extends her hand.*) Shake away.
RONNIE. Thanks. You know I regard your being here as nothing short of providential. Sometime when you have ten minutes to spare, may I talk to you? Get some advice?
LOUISE. What about?
RONNIE. The trouble is—here. (*He touches the top of his head.*) My scalp.
LOUISE. You sure you want *me?* I believe Fitch puts out a very good—
RONNIE. No, no. It isn't dandruff. It's— (*Looks around elaborately; then pretends to lower his voice.*) relatives.

(CORINNE'S *hands begin to clench.*)

LOUISE. Watch out, young man!
RONNIE. (*Still smiling.*) Don't you think it's tragic that a young man like myself—with so much to give—handsome, charming, talented—
LOUISE. Conceited—
RONNIE. Conceited—should be annoyed by anything—so rather disgusting as—relatives? As an expert in the gentle art of—murder, couldn't you show me some way to—er—?
LOUISE. Possibly. But my murderers always get caught. Anyone so handsome and talented—by the way, what is your talent?

RONNIE. I'm a composer. I've discovered a new wrinkle on the whole-tone scale—something Debussy and the others didn't think of.
LOUISE. Pity to hang you, then. I'd forget it.
RONNIE. Perhaps you're right. And it would be complicated, involving as it would, infanticide. I don't know whether my dear cousin has told you, told you, but— (*He turns to* CORINNE.) She has four of the choicest little— brats that—
CORINNE. (*Goes to him.*) You filthy, low-down, horrible beast! You—

(*As her fingers go to his throat, he simply takes her hands and holds them. And he laughs.*)

LOUISE. Let her go!

(*He releases* CORINNE, *who turns and runs blindly through Right arch to hall; she soon appears at Left arch; stands there a second; then she sees* MRS. SMYTHE.)

CORINNE. *You! You* here? What are you doing here? Answer me! What are you doing here? (*Calls loudly.*) Elizabeth! *Elizabeth!* (*To* MRS. SMYTHE.) Never mind! I'll find out!
MRS. SMYTHE. (*Beginning to show courage.*) I don't mind in the least.

(ELIZABETH *comes through swinging door. She has a pot of coffee in her hand.*)

CORINNE. Elizabeth! What's that woman doing here?
ELIZABETH. Corinne! What are you talking about?
CORINNE. How'd she get into this house?
ELIZABETH. Please! Mrs. Smythe is a guest here.
MRS. SMYTHE. I came with Mrs. Gensett.
CORINNE. I don't believe you. You're lying!
ELIZABETH. Stop it! It's perfectly true.

CORINNE. She came with Aunt Laura?

ELIZABETH. Yes. Yes, yes! In the car with Aunt Laura—and the nurse—and the chauffeur—and—whew! (*She puts coffee pot on table.*)

CORINNE. You fool! Don't you know who that woman is?

ELIZABETH. Corinne!

CORINNE. (*Her voice mounting.*) You mean you don't know? Then I'll tell you! She's a sly, sneaky little—

ELIZABETH. Stop it! Control yourself!

CORINNE. No! You're a fool, I tell you! That woman has a tiny apartment in Bridgeport. She met Aunt Laura in a tea-room—and latched onto her! And she's stayed latched!

ELIZABETH. If you don't keep quiet—

CORINNE. Ask her! Ask her! Every day she showed up at my house—to see "dear Mrs. Gensett"—mealy-mouthed creature! Don't you see what she's after? (ELIZABETH *suddenly takes hold of* CORINNE, *and shakes her.*) Let me go! Take your hands off me!

A MAN'S VOICE. (TOM BYRON, *heard in hallway at Right.*) What the hell's going on here? (*He is seen through living room arch, going from Right to Left.*)

RONNIE. Corinne's having a good one.

ELIZABETH. Tom! Is that you? Come help me!

TOM. Right. (*He has appeared at dining room arch.*)

CORINNE. Let me go, you sanctimonious old maid, you! You think I don't know what you—? You're nothing but a nasty, vicious old virgin!

TOM. Here—here—here!

CORINNE. (*Turns on him.*) And don't you touch me! Don't you put your filthy hands on me—you low rotten drunken bum! A *sot!* That's all you are! A *sot!* Wallowing in the—

(*But* TOM—*a tall man—has picked her up bodily; he carries her through the swinging doors,* CORINNE *screaming, fighting and kicking.*)

ACT I   A HOME FOR STRAY CATS   23

TOM. (*Offstage, as the door swings open.*) You bit me, you devil! (*As it swings open again.*) Head in the sink!

(*There is a pause.* ELIZABETH *sits at the table, and puts her head in her hands.*)

RONNIE. (*In Living Room.*) I have such sympathy for you poor people who live in New York. And I'm always so happy when one of you can escape—to the blessed peace of the countryside.

(RONNIE *sits, puts his hands behind his head, and leans back closing his eyes.* ELIZABETH *rises.*)

ELIZABETH. I'm deeply mortified, Mrs. Smythe, that you were put through—
MRS. SMYTHE. Please! It's *quite* all right. Everyone in Bridgeport understands—your poor cousin is unwell. But I do want to say—although Mrs. Gensett asked me to be her guest here—I'd rather not be thought of as—charity. (*She opens her bag and takes out some bills.*) So—one week's board. I'm fond of Mrs. Gensett—and she seems fond of me—and I wouldn't like anyone to—misunderstand. I think I'll say good night. (ELIZABETH *stands looking down at the money.* MRS. SMYTHE *goes to archway.*) Oh, my book—my book! (*She returns to table to get it.*) You know I've been cheating a little—reading on ahead. Ha, ha! (*Shakes a playful finger.*) But you mustn't tell dear Mrs. Gensett! They're in Rome now. Lord Claypool had to go there—something to do with the embassy. And now he and Antonia are going to meet by moonlight at—
HARRIET. (*Has appeared at Left arch.*) At the Colisco. That's the Coliseum. And St. Pietro is Pete—good old Pete! And Via is street—and fontana is fountain—and so on—and so on—etcetera!
MRS. SMYTHE. (*Her eyes flash dangerously for a second; then she decides to smile.*) How clever you are! You should really read this.

HARRIET. Yes, I really should. Sounds like the best seller for the year of nineteen hundred and six.

(MRS. SMYTHE *leaves Left archway.* HARRIET *looks towards* ELIZABETH, *who quietly goes out by swinging door.* HARRIET *sees coffee pot, goes to sideboard for a fresh cup and sits at table.* MRS. SMYTHE *appears at living room arch.*)

MRS. SMYTHE. Good night, Mrs. Vickers. And may I wish you—Ha, ha!—pleasant dreams?
LOUISE. Thank you. None at all would be better, though. Then I wouldn't mind so much getting up in the morning. (MRS. SMYTHE *is looking at* RONNIE.) Oh, this is Mr. Bliss—at least I *think* it's Mr. Bliss.
MRS. SMYTHE. (*She might like a chat.*) Oh, I've heard of you. How do you do?
RONNIE. (*Opens one eye, but doesn't move.*) How do you do? Good night.
MRS. SMYTHE. (*Miffed.*) Well! (*She disappears towards stairs.*)
RONNIE. (*Suddenly sitting up.*) Penny for your— No. One dollar and seventy-six cents for your thoughts. That's all I have with me. About all I have *not* with me, too.
LOUISE. Bad as that?
RONNIE. The world is not quite ready for my genius.
LOUISE. I see. And I suppose in the meantime electric dishwashers have made jobs hard to secure, hm.
RONNIE. Think of my pretty hands! (*He stretches out his strong, capable fingers in a sort of strangling movement.*)
LOUISE. A composer? If you'd said concert artist, now . . . You don't go around taking home movies of yourself composing, do you?
RONNIE. No. But it's an idea. I could show them to my grarrand arrant Laura. She says I don't work.
LOUISE. Oh, you do work?
RONNIE. Four hours every morning I spend in the

throes of creation. Chewing pencils—knocking my head against the piano—*you* should know!
LOUISE. I use an architect's table, white pine. It's softer.
RONNIE. In the afternoon I teach music at a girls' school. I have one pupil who puts her foot on the loud pedal—then puts the other foot on top of it to make it louder. Three nights a week I play piano at a charming little spot called "The Naked Angel"! It's not a place to go get a drink—you have to be drunk before you go there. Dancing in the front room—gambling in the back room—and upstairs—
LOUISE. Spare me. I'm sorry.
RONNIE. What are you sorry about?
LOUISE. I was . . . thinking of that poor woman in there.
RONNIE. Corinne? Yes. Tragic, isn't it? (*But he gives a jarring laugh.*) After the birth of her last child—it was one of those seven-month contraptions— (LOUISE *winces.* RONNIE *sees it, but simply smiles.*) she had a severe nervous breakdown.
LOUISE. And your idea is to see that she has another one, hm? The next time you're so blithely listing your attributes—handsome, charming, talented—add another, will you? Cruel.
RONNIE. (*Suddenly rises.*) Yeah? Well . . . let me tell you something. Cruelty lives by what it feeds on. Or, rather, by what is fed *to* it. My mother is dying—an operation would save her. Three times I've got that old hellion upstairs to the point of giving me a check. And three times some member of this precious family has got at her—and persuaded her not to sign it.
LOUISE. Oh, no.
RONNIE. That's why I'm here tonight—to get that check. I needed courage to tackle her. Our little talk has supplied it. (*He goes quickly to arch, and turns.*) I'm going to get that check tonight. (HARRIET, *in dining room, looks up, as she hears this.*) And I'll cut the living guts

out of anybody who interferes. And, now, may I, too, wish you pleasant dreams, Mrs. Vickers?

(*He goes towards stairs.* HARRIET *rises quickly, goes to hall; then appears at arch to living room.*)

LOUISE. You heard?
HARRIET. Yes, and I heard that crazy woman too.
LOUISE. Oh? Where were you?
HARRIET. On the stairs. I'd gone to get some cigarettes. You can hear everything in this house. Surely now you don't intend to stay, do you?
LOUISE. (*Holds up her wrists.*) Small bones. Stubborn.
HARRIET. Then for heaven's sake get a little good out of it! It's a perfect set-up. All you have to do is use it.
LOUISE. Set-up?
HARRIET. Yes, for murder. That old woman up there—who won't die—keeps everyone on tenterhooks. That young man who wants to cut people's guts out. That wild woman—she'd do anything to get money for those children of hers! Anything! That sap—with the book! "Blossom"! Ha! You don't think she's real, do you? A phony—if there ever was one. And the mistress of the house—
LOUISE. You don't like Elizabeth Byron, do you? Why?
HARRIET. Because she's a martyr! And I hate martyrs. Oh, so brave about it all! Ugh! She's a blood-sucker, too.
LOUISE. She's . . . And whose blood, may I ask, is she—?
HARRIET. Her brother's, for one. She's turned him into a drunkard. Not that it isn't his fault too. But—
LOUISE. You do get around, don't you?
HARRIET. Oh, everybody knows that. You heard that Corinne woman a while ago. You must have. She screamed it out!
LOUISE. I never listen to people when they scream. I flip a switch—and turn my ears off.
HARRIET. Too much of a lady?
LOUISE. Odd what you do with that word. You make it

sound like pickpocket or cattle thief. (*She starts for dining area.*)

HARRIET. Where are you going?

LOUISE. To get some of that coffee.

HARRIET. It'll keep you awake.

LOUISE. Oh, no. Not tonight. Two people have just wished me pleasant dreams. I shall probably go right off to sleep—and have one nightmare right after another.

HARRIET. (*She follows to dining area.*) Well, will you use it?

LOUISE. Certainly not. (*Gets fresh cup from sideboard.*)

HARRIET. Why not? All at each other's throats. Half a dozen characters all ready-made for you. And this old barn of a house—front stairs—back stairs—side stairs. Wings—halls—cross hall—high ceilings—half the place in shadows. What more do you want? Get a punch for the end of it—and it'll practically write itself. Well?

LOUISE. (*Is pouring coffee. She stops.*) Are you—serious? (*Looks at the* OTHER *in wonder.*) I believe you are.

HARRIET. Well, what's wrong with it? Oh, I know all that stuff in the front— "Characters—fictitious—any resemblance to living people," and so forth. But they won't sue. Make them unpleasant enough—they won't dare sue.

LOUISE. I wasn't thinking of a court of law.

HARRIET. What then?

LOUISE. I'm not in the habit of coming into someone's home and using the people I meet there as copy.

HARRIET. Well, you had your chance. Since you didn't take it, *I* will. Yes, I'll write it.

LOUISE. What?

HARRIET. Yes. That's what I said! Maybe you think I can't write one of those crazy crime things.

LOUISE. I never said any such thing. The reason I'm surprised is—on two or three occasions I've asked you if you ever felt any urge to write and you—

HARRIET. I never did before. But now I—

(*The swinging door opens, and* TOM *comes in carrying a*

plate on which there is a slab of cheese, some crackers and a long, sharp bread knife. Tom Byron *is only thirty, but already there have begun to develop in his face those almost indefinable, but unmistakable marks of dissipation. At his entrance,* Harriet *stiffens.*)

Tom. My supper. Would anyone care to share it with me?

Louise. (*Shakes her head.*) You missed an excellent dinner.

Tom. Oh, I'm rather an odd-times eater. An olive here—a salted peanut there.

Louise. How is—Mrs. Walker?

Tom. Spent. She makes everybody else suffer when she has one of these little—spells. Then, when it's over—

Louise. She suffers herself.

Tom. (*Nods.*) I'm sure something can be done about it, but—

Harriet. A little self-control might help, I should think.

Tom. Possibly. But since it's a commodity I'm sadly lacking in myself, I hardly like to suggest it.

Louise. (*With a glance at* Harriet.) It's a commodity we could all do with a little more of.

Tom. (*Clucks mockingly.*) Tch! Tch, tch! You've just ended a sentence with a preposition, Mrs. Vickers!

Louise. (*Playing along.*) Oh, no! Have I? What must you think of me!

Tom. I'll spend no more five cents a day reading fee on *you*, I can tell you. I must call up Fred. Corinne's in no condition to drive home.

Harriet. Couldn't you drive her?

Tom. I have no license.

Harriet. Oh, yes. I believe you told me this afternoon you'd—lost it.

Tom. Yes. I believe I did. Mrs. Vickers, I think I have an idea—about a place for you to work, I mean. It's a sort of store room, at the moment—in the old part of the house. But it has heat. I'll throw out the junk—put a rug down for you. I believe I can make it quite comfortable—that is, if you're staying.

LOUISE. I'm staying, Mr. Byron. My mind is quite made up.

TOM. You know—that makes me very happy.

LOUISE. Does it? Why?

TOM. Because I like you.

LOUISE. As simple as that?

TOM. As simple as that. Meantime—until I can get it fixed up—why not use this room?

LOUISE. Your dining room?

TOM. Why not? In the morning, anyway. The guests all have breakfast in their rooms. Oh, and at night, too. I don't know if you work at night—

HARRIET. *I* like to. If it isn't *too* much trouble. (*She gives him an odd look, then strides through Left arch, into hall, and to stairs.*)

LOUISE. (*Has noticed the look.*) You and Harriet took a walk this afternoon. I'm afraid it wasn't a success.

TOM. I'm afraid not. My fault. I took her to a place called "Rollo's Tavern." She didn't like it. So I brought her home.

LOUISE. I see.

TOM. I returned there. I—drink, you know.

LOUISE. Oh. Like it?

TOM. Not particularly.

LOUISE. Too bad. Seems a pity to have a vice—and not get any fun out of it. Why did you tell me this?

TOM. I've got into the habit somehow. A sort of—warning. And then—perhaps I get a kick out of cutting the ground from under people's feet. Just when they're getting ready to say, "You've been drinking," I say it.

LOUISE. Hm. I don't believe *I* should have said that, you know.

TOM. No. I don't believe you would. And therefore—I apologize. (ELIZABETH *comes through swinging doors. She has a tray on which are two small thermos jugs, each on a plate. One of the plates has crackers on it.*) Now what? Don't you ever get through with serving meals around this place?

ELIZABETH. Aunt Laura. And the nurse.

TOM. The *nurse?*

ELIZABETH. She's had two cups of black coffee, to keep her awake. Now she wants ovaltine— to put her to sleep.

TOM. Hmph! The nurse waits on the patient—and it takes four people to wait on the nurse. Give it to me.

ELIZABETH. No, Tom. No. I want you to *eat.* You've eaten nothing all day and you—

TOM. All right—all right.

ELIZABETH. You promised you— Please, Mrs. Vickers. Make the man eat something, will you?

TOM. I said all right. (*He picks up his plate of cheese.*)

ELIZABETH. Did you call up Fred?

TOM. I'll do it right away.

LOUISE. That's a lot of knife for so little cheese.

(*She points at it.* TOM *smiles and takes it with him into hall.*)

RONNIE. (*His angry voice heard in hall.*) All right—all right—all right!

TOM. What's the matter, Ronnie?

RONNIE. Damned nurse! Wouldn't let me in!

ELIZABETH. (*To* LOUISE.) I've sent Martha to help Corinne to bed. Now I've got to tackle that nurse for something to keep her quiet.

(RONNIE *appears at living room arch.*)

LOUISE. Don't. I have something. They're right here in —no, my bag's in the living room.

ELIZABETH. Oh, may I get them?

LOUISE. Help yourself. Pretty weak, I'm afraid. The fussy old doctor of mine thinks I'm a potential dope-fiend. I have to practically bite him to get an aspirin tablet. Oh, Miss Byron. They're the ones in the *small* phial.

(Elizabeth *has moved Downstage and goes to living room area. She is still carrying the tray. She puts down tray on coffee table, goes to chair where* Louise *left her bag and picks up bag.* Louise *sits at dining room table with her small pad. She makes a note.*)

Elizabeth. I'm not engaged in larceny. Mrs. Vickers said I might have one of these for Corinne. (*She extracts a small phial.*)
Ronnie. Rather have some of this? (*He produces a bottle from his pocket, wrapped in paper.*) The doctor gave it to me, for Mother. She can't take tablets.
Elizabeth. Pretty strong, I imagine. Isn't it? (Ronnie *shrugs.*) This will do. (*She puts one tablet on tray and replaces phial.*) How *is* your mother, Ronnie? (*He shakes his head.*) I'm sorry.
Ronnie. Wait! I don't like that new nurse. And there's something about her—
Elizabeth. I wonder if you're thinking what I'm thinking. A spy.
Ronnie. "Spy"? What do you— Oh, you mean for Cousin George?
Elizabeth. (*Nods.*) To look after his interests. She came on the case when Aunt Laura was at George's house. He could have made some—well, arrangement with her. George writes his "dear aunt"—absolute poems of love and affection. The nurse reads them to the old lady. How easy to slip in a good word like "Now, *he's* nice!" "So devoted to you!" And so forth.
Ronnie. I never thought of that. Give me that tray. I'll take it up for you.
Elizabeth. No, no. I—
Ronnie. Give it to me! Save you a few steps. (*He takes it from her.*)
Elizabeth. The maid's with Corinne. You can give her the tablet. (Ronnie *starts.*) Oh. Just set the thermos bottles outside their doors. Aunt Laura's and the nurse's. The one with the crackers on it is Aunt Laura's.

RONNIE. I know. She eats like a stevedore.
ELIZABETH. (*Smiles.*) She's an invalid.
RONNIE. Yeah. At our house she has five square meals—a midnight snack—and at six A.M. she starts yelling for ham and eggs.

(*He goes through arch, and to stairs.* ELIZABETH *holds it a second; then, rather wearily, starts for hall.*)

TOM. (*Offstage, in hall.*) All right, Fred. Take care of yourself. . . . Yes . . . we'll look after her. Good night. (*As* ELIZABETH *reaches hall.*) You've had a long day. Why don't you turn in? (*He comes within view of arch.*)
ELIZABETH. I think I will. I hope *you* get some rest. I hate your being turned out of your room.
TOM. (*Puts an arm around her affectionately.*) The back hall suits me fine. I'm up and down all night anyway.
ELIZABETH. I know— I know! That's what—
TOM. Forget it. (*He gives her a peck on the cheek, and pushes her towards rear.* LOUISE, *at dining room table, suddenly thinks of something else, and makes a brief note on her pad.* TOM *appears at Left archway.*) Am I interrupting?
LOUISE. Not a bit of it. This is the time of day I usually write little notes to myself.
TOM. Oh? I've never tried that. Of course I talk to myself a good deal but— What do you say? Or is that a trade secret?
LOUISE. Oh—things like: "Try reversing it. Kill Horace first; *then*, Gertrude."
TOM. Sounds a bit bloodthirsty.
LOUISE. Well, murder is my business. Then I jot down little items like—shot gun too noisy—use meat cleaver.
TOM. Please. I've got to sleep on a cot in the back hall. And there's absolutely no way to lock myself in.
LOUISE. I'll remember that. Now this one says— (*Squints at it.*) Hm. What *does* it say? My glasses are in my . . . Here! (*She pushes it across to him.*)

ACT I   A HOME FOR STRAY CATS   33

Tom. (*Reading.*) "Stern Brothers." You're not killing off the Stern Brothers, are you?

Louise. (*Laughs.*) No. That's something else. I bought some gloves there the other day. A sale. It was crowded—and I got back the wrong charge-o-plate.

Tom. (*Flips a page.*) And this one says: "Could you possibly murder someone just because—?"

Louise. (*Quickly.*) No, no! Not that one!

Tom. Sorry. (*He pushes the pad across to her.*)

Louise. I didn't mean that. It's just . . . an idea that came to me tonight and—well, it's so crazy cockeyed that—

Mrs. Smythe. (*She appears at Left archway.*) Mrs. Vickers, dear Mrs. Gensett would like to speak to you.

Louise. To *me?*

Mrs. Smythe. Yes. I just dropped in to say good night to her. I told her this afternoon that we— Ha, ha!—had a very distinguished author staying here. Or is it "authoress"?

Louise. (*A bit annoyed.*) Really, Mrs. Smythe, you shouldn't have said that. I'm not distinguished and—

Mrs. Smythe. Oh, but you are. I'm sure you are! Ha, ha! Just because *I'm* not familiar with your—lovely books, doesn't mean that—

Ronnie. (*His voice in hall.*) Good night. Good night, all.

Tom. (*Calls.*) Oh, good night, Ronnie.

(Ronnie *is seen briefly through wide arch, on his way to Right. The front DOOR slams.*)

Mrs. Smythe. She says she'd be most grateful, if you could spare her a few minutes. (*She goes into hall towards stairs.*)

Louise. Thank you. (*To* Tom.) I suppose that's in the nature of a—summons?

Tom. No reason why *you* should obey it though. You're not in the sweepstakes.

Louise. I wonder what she wants.

Tom. Hm. How are you on witnessing wills?

LOUISE. Wills?

TOM. She keeps a whole drawerful of will-forms. About every twenty minutes, she tears up the old will and makes out a new one.

LOUISE. Not really?

TOM. She cuts out Elizabeth and me—and puts in Corinne. The next day Corinne's out—and it all goes to Ronnie's mother—or Cousin George.

LOUISE. Cousin George? I haven't met him, have I?

TOM. God forbid. If you do, hang on to your piggy bank. He lives in Norwalk and he's a complete bastard. The irony of it is that, in the end, none of us will get it. The two million will go to supplying catnip to retired alley cats.

LOUISE. Two million? Why doesn't she split it up among the lot of you?

TOM. You don't know Aunt Laura. That wouldn't give her anything to laugh about—in the cemetery.

LOUISE. How awful! Two million, that amount of money—even a *small* amount of money—can do so much good. In the hands of the right people.

TOM. And who would you say were the right people?

LOUISE. I don't know. I haven't thought it out. Offhand I'd say people with sympathy, understanding, pity, I don't know. (*Rising.*) Well—if needs must—you know the last time I was summoned like this—it was an old man in Florida. In the middle of the night he sent for me and asked me quite seriously if I could suggest some way for him to get rid of his two step-daughters.

TOM. Nothing like being an expert! I suppose you get letters?

LOUISE. All the time. "Will cyanide cure my husband of snoring?" "My wife burned our roast again. How much is a sashweight?" I've often thought of starting a column—"Lizzie Borden Blake" or—"Dear Lucretia Fairfax."

(*As she moves towards arch, the LIGHTS dim.*)

THE CURTAIN FALLS

ACT TWO

Scene 1

Scene: *The LIGHTS are on in the hall. The single table LAMP is on in the living room. In the dining room, the wall brackets have been turned off, only the DROP LIGHT over the table is burning. There is only one change in the set. On the dining-room table is a portable typewriter. A stack of yellow second-sheets are on the table beside it, and there is a double-sheet, but not carbon, in the typewriter. Someone has been typing and has reached to nearly the end of the page in single-space.*

At Rise: *The Stage is empty.* Martha, *the maid, comes from the rear of hall, to arch to living room. She seems uncertain and rather furtive in her movements. She looks at her wrist watch. Then she hears a slight NOISE. She looks around to be sure she is not observed; then she goes to French window in the living room, and unfastens the catch.* Ronnie *glides quickly into the room, and* Martha *closes the window behind her, but does not fasten the catch.*

Martha. This is insane! Crazy!
Ronnie. Sh—h!
Martha. Why did you have to come back? Why? *Why?*
Ronnie. Keep your voice down! I told you why. I've got to have a few minutes with the old lady, without anybody barging in.
Martha. And what makes you think they won't barge in?

RONNIE. She's gone to bed.

MARTHA. Yeah? Well, nobody else has. That secretary woman—here with that writer—I just met her in the back passage—she had a piece of paper in her hand. What the hell's she doing roaming around like that?

RONNIE. I don't even know what you're talking about.

MARTHA. And that crazy cousin—I put her to bed but she won't stay there. Your whole damned family's crazy, if you ask me. Including Elizabeth.

RONNIE. Now, now—there's nothing wrong with—

MARTHA. She's not human. She doesn't walk. She just appears. You go round a corner—and there she is! Not a sound! But there she is! She scares the living daylights out of me! I wish I'd never come here.

RONNIE. But you are here. It's only for a few days.

MARTHA. Damned tootin' it's only for a few days. This old house—wings and stairways—nooks and crannies—shadows all over the—

RONNIE. All right—all right! Never mind. Now listen! Here's what I want you to do. Put that hall light out.

MARTHA. Why can't you turn it off?

RONNIE. Not turn it off. Put it out. It's a ceiling light. At the top of the stairs, there's a curtained alcove. Go in there—lean way over the bannister—and you can just reach it. Unscrew the bulb—and take it away with you.

MARTHA. You were up there. Why didn't you—?

RONNIE. Not at that hour. Tom—or somebody—would put in another one. This late, they won't bother.

MARTHA. Suppose somebody sees me?

RONNIE. It's got a curtain across it. Nobody *can* see you—except someone looking up from downstairs.

MARTHA. But getting there—or coming away—?

RONNIE. Suppose they do? You're the maid, aren't you? You left a tray—or you forgot to put out fresh towels. Use your head!

MARTHA. Don't you talk to me that way!

RONNIE. (*Slipping an arm around her.*) I'm sorry, sweet, but—

MARTHA. (*Freeing herself.*) And none of that "sweet" stuff!
RONNIE. What's the matter with you?

(*He suddenly seizes her wrist to keep her quiet. He has heard something. He darts towards window.* MARTHA *extracts a spoon from the pocket of her uniform, throws it on the floor near a chair, and kneels down to pick it up, just as* TOM *appears briefly at Right archway. He is carrying a set of portieres.*)

MARTHA. I dropped this. I thought I'd better get it before morning.
TOM. I see. Thank you. (*We don't know if he accepts this explanation or not. But he moves towards Left, out of sight.* RONNIE *waits, then leaves window. He makes signs at* MARTHA, *pointing up, and the motion of unscrewing a bulb.* TOM *comes through arch into dining room. He gets a chair from table, puts it near arch and climbs on it. The portieres are already on a pole and the hooks already on the wall. He steps down, adjusts portieres, so that they almost meet in the Center, replaces chair, and sits at table, lighting a cigarette.* MARTHA *hurries out into hall, and towards stairs.* RONNIE *goes close to arch, but is careful not to appear in the view of anyone in hall. He waits impatiently. Then the LIGHT goes out in the hall. As it does we hear a* WOMAN'S *voice saying sharply* "Oh!" *There is, of course, a "spill" into hall from the lights in the living room. Soon we see* LOUISE *in hall, groping her way. Then she moves out of sight, Left of arch.* LOUISE *comes through portieres into dining room. She gives the portieres a cursory glance, no more, as she is obviously upset over something.* TOM *rises, nods towards portieres.*) Happened to think of those. We use them in very cold weather. I thought they'd give you a little privacy. (LOUISE *moves to sideboard, and leans against it. She turns and looks at* TOM.) Anything wrong? (*She doesn't answer for a second.* RONNIE *darts out into darkened hall*

and towards stairs.) You're looking at me as if . . . Have I done something that—?

LOUISE. No. *You* haven't done anything. I—I've had a bit of a shock.

TOM. What kind of—? Are you all right? (*She nods.*) You haven't been with Aunt Laura all this time?

LOUISE. No. In my room. I had to think something out. As a matter of fact I didn't see your aunt.

TOM. You didn't see her?

LOUISE. No. The nurse ushered me into the room. Your aunt wasn't there. I heard the water running so I assume she was in the bathroom.

TOM. And you didn't wait?

LOUISE. No. Because of something I saw. I— (*For the first time she becomes really conscious of the typewriter on the dining room table. She nods towards it.*) Harriet?

TOM. I guess so.

LOUISE. Where is she? (TOM *shrugs, shakes his head.*) You say you're a drinker? Secret drinker? How secret?

TOM. Well, not "top" secret. It's pretty generally known throughout Connecticut. I don't know about Rhode Island and Massachusetts.

LOUISE. You mean you're the kind who hides bottles in laundry baskets—places like that?

TOM. How did you know?

LOUISE. Do you think you could find one of those bottles now—pour me out two good slugs, with a little plain water?

TOM. You mean that? Move, then.

LOUISE. I beg your pardon.

TOM. I said move. Sit down over there.

LOUISE. Can't I stand up at the bar?

TOM. Not if you get in the way of the bartender. (*He grins, and gently moves her to one side. Then he reaches in bottom drawer of sideboard and pulls out some table linen. He comes up with a very handsome tablecloth and from its folds extracts a pint bottle of whiskey.*)

LOUISE. Imagine! Penniless beggar—and I was leaning against Fort Knox.

TOM. We only use this tablecloth for Thanksgiving and Christmas. (*Pouring a drink in a clean glass from sideboard.*) Would you like to say "When"?

LOUISE. Just a nice good ladylike drink—then double it. Aren't you going to have one?

TOM. I was hoping you'd ask me. (*He fixes his neat.*) What would you like to drink to?

LOUISE. *I* shall drink to my own colossal stupidity. But you needn't. (*She looks at him.*) On your aunt's dresser are a great many photographs.

TOM. The whole family. Amazing—when she dislikes us so much—she travels about with cabinet-sized pictures of us. I have an idea she gets up in the middle of the night and throws darts at them.

LOUISE. The one of you is a blown-up snapshot. I've seen that snapshot before.

TOM. You—wait a minute. You've seen a picture—of *me?* In some—post office? "This man is dangerous—"

LOUISE. Some time ago, at a restaurant, I accidentally picked up Harriet's compact instead of my own.

TOM. (*Takes a long pull at his drink. There is a pause.*) I see. I never imagined somehow I'd make a compact. (*Another pause.*) You're—not going to ask *me* about this, are you?

LOUISE. No. You wouldn't tell me anyway. But I'm certainly going to ask Harriet. She's placed me in a very embarrassing position.

TOM. Yes. I can see that. But— I'm sure she didn't mean to—

LOUISE. Loyal, Mr. Byron?

TOM. In my feeble way. (*He smiles.*) You'll find I have all the outmoded virtues.

LOUISE. (*She, too, smiles.*) You know I rather guessed that about you. Loyal—and—tell me, are you brave?

TOM. An absolute lion. I can take on a whole tank corps before breakfast—but I'm scared as hell to look at my own face while I'm shaving. (*He is near portieres, which are almost but not quite closed; he happens to look out, then he opens them a bit wider.*) Strange. Wonder who put the light out in the hall.

LOUISE. The maid, I think. We passed each other on the stairs. Just as I got to the bottom, she turned it off, from above.

TOM. Oh, no. Not from above. It's not a two-way switch. (*He goes through arch into hall.* LOUISE *idly sits at table with her drink. She is by typewriter.* TOM *passes wide living room arch, going to Right of it.* LOUISE *starts to read the yellow sheet in typewriter. She is outraged by what she reads. She suddenly rises, extracting the paper from the machine.* TOM *passes wide arch, on way back, and comes through portieres Left.*) Bulb must have burned out.

LOUISE. Mr. Byron, did you read this? It was in the typewriter.

TOM. No. Certainly not.

LOUISE. Forgive me. I shouldn't have asked. But, please. Has this room been empty?

TOM. It was empty when I came in to hang those things. (*Nods towards portieres.*)

LOUISE. And Harriet? You don't know where Harriet is?

(*The swinging door has just opened.*)

HARRIET. Here's Harriet. What do you want with her? (*Then she sees the yellow sheet in* LOUISE'S *hand; she looks quickly at typewriter.*) That's mine! Give it to me!

LOUISE. No.

HARRIET. (*Advancing on her.*) Yes. It's mine, I tell you! You had no right to look at it. Give it to me!

(LOUISE *looks at her a second, then folds the sheet once, and extends it.* HARRIET *seizes it, and the two women confront each other.*)

TOM. Would you—like me to go? (*Without even looking at him,* LOUISE *nods slightly. He moves towards swinging door.*) I'll see if I can find another bulb for that—
LOUISE. Please don't bother. I'll go up the back way.

(*He quietly goes out. There is a pause.*)

HARRIET. A while ago when I told you what I was going to do, you didn't believe me, did you? (LOUISE *shakes her head.*) Well, I'm going to do it. And I've got it all worked out. I'm going to kill that old woman upstairs—smother her with a pillow. First though I'll get the nurse out of the way—sleeping pills or something. Then . . . Why are you looking at me like that? You don't think I can do it? Maybe I can't, but I'm certainly going to try. (*Suddenly in alarm, holding out yellow paper.*) How much of this did you read?
LOUISE. Quite enough. Thumbnail sketches of your characters.
HARRIET. You didn't read the end, where I put down the—
LOUISE. The "wallop"? Are you afraid I'll steal it from you?
HARRIET. Well—no, but—
LOUISE. You left that paper in the typewriter. You went out of the room.
HARRIET. (*Alluding to the white piece of paper in her hand.*) I was making a plan of the house.
LOUISE. For whatever reason, you left it there. Anyone could have come in and read it. You described your characters in the most venomous terms—and you didn't even change the names.
HARRIET. Of course I'll have to change their names.
LOUISE. You didn't bother to on that. Since everyone here knows you are employed as my secretary the natural conclusion would be you were writing for *me*. I resent that very much. And I resent, too, your getting me here under false pretense. Yes. I asked you to find a quiet place in

the country. You came to me with the name "Linden Lodge." When I asked you what you knew about it, you said nothing. That was a deliberate falsehood. You knew *all* about it. And you knew at least one person here. What you and Tom Byron were to each other—

HARRIET. Didn't he tell you?

LOUISE. Certainly not. He told me nothing.

HARRIET. Ha! Too much the gentleman, hm?

LOUISE. I like gentlemen.

HARRIET. I know you do. It's an absolute fetish with you. Well, maybe you'd like to hear about *this* one.

LOUISE. I don't think so. I'm no longer interested. I shall be leaving first thing in the morning. You may do as you please. And I think it only fair to tell you that— I'm afraid our usefulness to each other is at an end.

HARRIET. In other words, I'm fired.

LOUISE. Since you prefer things being put in the crudest possible manner—yes! (*She starts for swinging door.*)

HARRIET. All right—all right. But wait!

LOUISE. I see no point in—

HARRIET. You pride yourself on being fair—*just*—but you won't even listen to me.

LOUISE. Very well. I'm listening.

HARRIET. Tom Byron and I were engaged. He was working in New York. It wasn't much of a job—he's not a money-maker. But that was all right. Then one day he came to me—said he couldn't marry me—or anybody. His— (*With great scorn.*) sister needed him. This place was heavily mortgaged. She'd lose it unless she turned it into a glorified boarding house. But she couldn't run it alone. Too big. And she couldn't pay people. He gave me up to come up here and cut the grass—shovel snow—feed the pigs—if they *have* pigs! Always I wanted to *see* this place. An excuse to get here. Oh, don't think I wanted *him* back! God, I wouldn't have him. But I wanted to see this—sister of his. This marvelous sister—that he was so *devoted* to. That he loved so—it amounted almost to incest!

LOUISE. Look out! Someone will hear you!
HARRIET. Do you think I care? Well, I've seen her. And I've seen what she's turned him into. Hitting the bottle because he's bored stiff. And I've seen some of the rest of the family. And they're not worth a damn. Any of them. They've got only one thought in their heads. "When's that old woman up there going to die—so I can get my greedy hands on her money!" The strain they live under. One of them—Corinne—has already cracked. But they're *all* ready to crack. Can you think up a better murder set-up than this? Well?
LOUISE. (*After a pause.*) How you've changed! So bitter! So— I'm very sorry for you, Harriet. Not so much for what Tom Byron did to you but for what you're doing to yourself. (*Lowering her voice.*) I wouldn't leave my notes lying about if I were you. If, as you say, some of the people in this house are about to crack, your notes might give one of them an idea. The murder on paper might turn into reality.

(*She goes out through swinging door.* HARRIET *looks after her; then goes to typewriter. She puts the piece of yellow paper on the table beside it. Then from a stack of yellow paper, she takes a sheet and inserts it in the roll. She sits. She thinks a minute, then types. She stops, thinks again, and lights a cigarette. Then she types some more, fast and furiously. Suddenly she breaks off and looks up. She has heard something. Not sure where this very slight noise comes from, she looks around. She hears it again, and traces it to just outside the curtained archway.*)

HARRIET. Yes? . . . Yes? (*She rises. She speaks sharply.*) Who is it? Who's out there? (*She moves towards archway.*) Who's out there? What do you want? God, I hate this damned house and everybody in it!

(*There is a bulge in the curtain; something goes through.*

HARRIET *lets out a gasping sound. She puts her left hand to her breast; with her right she clutches at the portieres for support. The gasp changes into a sort of gurgle. Something flashes through the curtain again; and strikes her. She lets go the portieres, and turns. As she does so we see a dark blotch on her white blouse. Partly doubled over, she stumbles towards Left. She grabs wildly at a chair for support, but misses it; she sinks to her knees; then all the way down, turning and falling on her back. A count of three, then:*)

THE CURTAIN FALLS

(*The Curtain remains down 30 seconds, then rises again.*)

ACT TWO

SCENE 2

TIME: *Fifteen minutes later.*

AT RISE: LOUISE *is seated at the table by typewriter looking down.* TOM *has just spread the "Thanksgiving" table cover over* HARRIET's *body.* [NOTE: *We don't see the body again. So a dummy is used. The body, incidentally, is at Right of table and partially under it. There is just room for a person to reach the arch and go out through the portieres.*] *The LIGHTS are the same; the drop light in dining room is on; as are also the two table lamps in the living room. The hall is dark, as it was.*

TOM. I suppose it was all right to cover her.
LOUISE. I think so. So long as you don't touch the—body. . . . You *didn't*, did you?
TOM. No, why should I?
LOUISE. (*Nervously.*) Oh, no reason! I didn't mean

anything. I— I'm considered rather good at making up these situations. I find the reality a bit . . . I was fond of Harriet. I'm sorry that she—

TOM. Was—murdered?

LOUISE. (*Shudders.*) That, naturally. But I was thinking of—something else. You'd better call the police, hadn't you?

TOM. In a minute. Some things I'd like to get straightened out. In my own mind, I mean. (*She looks at him oddly.*) Surely a few minutes won't make any difference.

LOUISE. It's an established rule, Mr. Byron, to call the police at once.

TOM. It's a rule I intend to break. I'd like to know: When did you find her?

LOUISE. About five minutes before you walked through that door there. (*She points to swinging door.*) I—I started to get undressed. But I didn't. I was very upset, I was afraid I couldn't sleep. Then I remembered I had some sleeping tablets. In this. (*She holds up her bag.*) I'd left it downstairs.

TOM. You came in this way? (*He turns towards Left arch.*)

LOUISE. No. Through the other doorway. That's where my bag was. Then I realized I didn't hear the typewriter. I wondered. I was not particularly anxious to see Harriet again. We'd had some—words. But I came in here and . . . What are you looking at?

TOM. (*Has gone to archway.*) These drapes. There are some tears in them. Also—something that looks like—blood.

LOUISE. Please!

TOM. Sorry. I had no idea you were so squeamish.

LOUISE. I talk about it quite glibly, don't I? I don't feel quite so—glib now. I . . . Wait a minute! You mean—whoever did this . . . didn't come into the room to kill her, but—?

TOM. Stabbed her through the curtains. Probably called out to her—and when she was near—

LOUISE. Then she probably didn't even know who—

TOM. (*Examining drapes.*) He must have struck at her at least four times.

LOUISE. Why four times?

TOM. He was doing it blind. I guess he wanted to make sure.

LOUISE. Odd. So much easier to come into the room—and make sure that way. (*He suddenly goes out into the hall.*) What are you doing?

TOM. (*In hall.*) Damn that light. (*From outside, he opens up the portieres.*)

LOUISE. You shouldn't do that!

TOM. (*Just outside in hall.*) I've done it!

LOUISE. What are you looking for?

TOM. (*In hall.*) The knife. The knife I left on this telephone table with my cheese and crackers. It isn't here. And it wasn't dropped here. At least I don't see it. (*He returns to dining room and closes drapes.*)

LOUISE. Seems rather stupid to carry a thing like that away with him.

TOM. Even more stupid, I should think, to leave it around—if it had prints.

LOUISE. With the tons of literature on crime, nobody would leave fingerprints. We don't even think of them any more. (*She moves Downstage and towards living room.*)

TOM. Not *everyone* reads crime stories.

LOUISE. I really think, Mr. Byron, you should call the po—

TOM. Not yet. I don't intend to be arrested for this, if I can help it.

LOUISE. I see. Meaning *you* are the only person in this house who knew Harriet.

TOM. Except yourself, of course.

LOUISE. Except myself, yes. I didn't kill her, Mr. Byron.

TOM. And I didn't kill her either, Mrs. Vickers.

LOUISE. I never said you did.

Tom. No. And you may not even think so—at the moment. But the more you roll the idea around in your head, the more you're liable to think so. When you questioned Harriet tonight, I don't know what she told you—

Louise. She said you were engaged.

Tom. Anything else?

Louise. Some other things—yes. But—

Tom. (*An odd smile.*) That's all right. You needn't tell me. But the fact that we were—engaged—the fact that she had my picture in her compact—the fact that she was a complete stranger to everyone else in this household—makes me a number one suspect. And, of course, I could have done it quite simply. My couch is in the back hall—only a few steps away. It's fairly dark out there— (*He nods towards archway.*) but I could have easily found the knife on the telephone table, since I put it there myself. *And* I was the one who put up those drapes. (*He moves down and to Right.*)

Louise. Rather damning, isn't it?

Tom. Decidedly so. The only compensating fact is that *you* are the only person who knows all that. (*Moving closer to her.*)

Louise. I beg your pardon.

Tom. (*Goes closer still.*) You are the only one who knows I was engaged to Harriet—that she had my picture in her compact—that I put up the drapes as a possible screen—and noticed and remarked on the oversize knife.

Louise. Hm. If I were writing this, I'd say—something like—"At this point Louise Vickers suddenly raised a large crop of goose-pimples. She found herself alone with the murderer and realized she knew too much. Frightened out of her wits"—such as they are—"she slowly backed away from the murderer—" (*She does so.*) "until the back of her trembling knees collided with a chair—" (*She acts this out too.*) "and collapsed—too terrified even to scream." (*She sits.*) I—I wonder if I c-can scream.

Tom. Don't. Not until you hear the rest of it.

Louise. There's more?

Tom. This murderer isn't going to do it quite like that.
Louise. You're not?
Tom. No. I have another idea. We've done "Suspect Number One." Let's take up "Number Two." You. The only *other* person in this house who knew Harriet—and therefore who could have any conceivable reason for killing her. You and I are in the same boat, you know.
Louise. Oh, no. I'm not in a boat with anybody. I don't *like* boats. I get seasick.
Tom. Oh, but you are.
Louise. But I had no possible reason for wanting to kill Harriet.
Tom. But I happen to know you had. Or one which just *might* interest the police. Even back in the days I was going with Harriet in New York, she told me she was tired of working for you—that she wanted to branch out and be a mystery writer herself.
Louise. Why didn't she? All she had to do——
Tom. Wait. She said she'd learned a lot. That she'd done quite a bit of research for you—toxicology, ballistics, police procedure—that kind of thing. When she learned a bit more she was going to tell you to go to hell. *Nil nisi bonum,* Mrs. Vickers, but Harriet was pretty much—of a —well—
Louise. *Nil nisi bonum*—but, say it. Bitch. I'm just beginning to find that out.
Tom. I found that out some time ago. That's why— Never mind. Harriet was rather fond of self-analysis. She said her approach to writing was much more modern than yours. Her ideas were—forgive me—younger.
Louise. Quite all right.
Tom. That she'd learned from you how to build up suspense—things like that. Her one great weakness was characterization. She couldn't "create" people—when she did they didn't have flesh and blood. She could describe people if they existed—and she knew them. But she couldn't make them up.

ACT II A HOME FOR STRAY CATS

Louise. And tonight she found a lot of ready-made characters and—

Tom. What's that?

Louise. Nothing. Please go on. What are you trying to say, Mr. Byron? That I was jealous of Harriet?

Tom. Partially that and—

Louise. Rather far-fetched, don't you think?

Tom. It's not what I think. It's what the police might think.

Louise. Oh, no. Unless you have more to go on than that—

Tom. I have. My sister told me that Harriet was rather —taunting you this evening because you had a book to write—and didn't even have an idea.

Louise. Quite true. But I don't see—

Tom. Wait. Harriet came in tonight just after I'd poured our drinks. Remember? I'd only had a couple of swallows. I left. But I wanted that drink. Only I didn't want to interrupt. Then I thought of—er—another—

Louise. Hiding place?

Tom. An old umbrella stand in the hall out there. I slipped along quietly. I wasn't trying to listen, Mrs. Vickers. Please believe me. Whatever Harriet told you about me was quite all right.

Louise. But you did listen.

Tom. Not to that part. And I didn't listen. I overheard. Something about a wallop. "How much of this did you read?" "Do you think I'd steal your plot?" I can't quote the exact words, but—

Louise. You needn't. I get it. An elderly mystery-story writer—written out, perhaps—jealous of her younger secretary who also wants to write. The older woman has a book to do—but no idea for it. She's desperate. She discovers that her secretary *does* have an idea—which foolishly she puts down on a piece of yellow paper and so— Kkkkkk!

Tom. The piece of yellow paper is missing, Mrs. Vickers. Or didn't you notice?

LOUISE. As a matter of fact I did notice. Yes.

TOM. You didn't say anything about it.

LOUISE. I notice a great many things I don't say anything about. Is that your case against me, Mr. Byron?

TOM. Not quite.

LOUISE. My God! Soon you'll say you saw me with the knife in my hand.

TOM. Not the knife. The yellow paper. A few minutes ago you opened your bag to take out a cigarette. I saw the yellow paper.

LOUISE. (*Unconsciously her grip tightens on her bag.*) No. You saw yellow paper—but not *the* yellow paper. I buy that paper by the ream—by the ton. You saw me tonight with a small pad. I told you I wrote notes to myself. Well, I misplaced that pad—so wanting something to make notes on I grabbed some yellow paper and— Oh, you don't believe me?

TOM. Will you let me see the yellow paper you have in there now?

LOUISE. I certainly will not. I see no reason why I should. What is this, anyway? What are you—? Oh. Blackmail, hm? If I don't tell the police what I know, you won't tell them what you know.

TOM. That's the idea.

LOUISE. But that's ridiculous. They're obliged to find out about you and Harriet. They'll communicate with the police in New York and—

TOM. No. In New York Harriet and I never met at *her* place. Just at mine. I had a place in the Village—a basement flat with its own entrance. The other places we met were impersonal, like theatres—hotel lobbies—museums.

LOUISE. But the snapshot I saw—there may have been others too.

TOM. I don't think so. Harriet was not a sentimental person. And when we broke up I feel pretty sure she destroyed everything she had which might have reminded her of me. I left a pretty sour taste with her. So the only possible way to connect Harriet with me is through you. Well—is it a bargain?

LOUISE. Hm. I wish I knew the real reason for your wanting to make the bargain. It isn't for the reason you say at all. I know that, but I don't—

(*She is interrupted by a SCREAM, which comes from off and up. A second's pause and* TOM *hurries out through Right arch into hall.*)

TOM. (*Offstage, calling.*) What is it? What's the matter? (A WOMAN'S VOICE *calls out some unintelligible words.*) Be right up!

(LOUISE *quickly opens her bag, extracts a single folded sheet of yellow paper. She starts to tear it; then looks around, there is no place to put the pieces. She hurries to table in the dining room, the one with the typewriter on it. She grabs a bunch of yellow sheets from the stack, slips her own piece in the middle of the clean ones, folds them twice and returns them to her bag. She is just entering living area, when:*)

ELIZABETH. (*Her voice in hall.*) What is it? Who screamed?

LOUISE. (*Calling.*) Miss Byron!

ELIZABETH. (*She appears at Right archway.*) Someone screamed. Was it you?

LOUISE. It came from upstairs. Your brother's gone to— (ELIZABETH *starts to turn.*) No, wait, please. Your room's on this floor, isn't it?

ELIZABETH. Yes. Across—and off a small hallway. Why?

LOUISE. There's been an—accident, Miss Byron. A very serious one. And not really an accident. Miss Beam. She's dead. She was—stabbed. Probably with a knife your brother left on the telephone table.

ELIZABETH. (*Moves Downstage.*) Where — is — ?

(LOUISE *nods towards Left.* ELIZABETH *goes towards Left, looks Upstage, but does not enter dining area. Then she turns back.*) Is that why you asked me where my room was? I'm afraid it was quite apparent I didn't like Miss Beam, but not to the extent of . . . No, Mrs. Vickers. I didn't kill her.

LOUISE. I was asking because I thought you might have heard something, being so close by. (ELIZABETH *shakes her head.*) Were you asleep?

ELIZABETH. Well— I was reading—and I must have dozed. As a matter of fact, I think I did doze. Yes.

MRS. SMYTHE. (*Appears at Right arch, very much upset. She's wearing a frilly negligee.*) Oh, oh! I've never been so frightened in my life.

LOUISE. Was that you that screamed?

MRS. SMYTHE. Did I? I know I tried to. But I wasn't sure I made it.

LOUISE. You made it. What happened?

MRS. SMYTHE. Oh, a—a—a—man!

LOUISE. What?

MRS. SMYTHE. A man. Hurrying along the back hall.

ELIZABETH. Upstairs? What sort of a man?

MRS. SMYTHE. I couldn't see. Just his back. And there was only a night light.

ELIZABETH. Where did he go?

MRS. SMYTHE. Around the bend—or a corner—or something. I was just coming out of the bathroom.

ELIZABETH. Maybe he came down the backstairs. (*She starts off.*)

LOUISE. I wouldn't, Miss Byron. (ELIZABETH *stops.*)

MRS. SMYTHE. Oh, dear, I'm a teetotaler. I never take anything with an alcoholic content. Never. Never! But this is one of those times— (*To* ELIZABETH.) Do you happen to have a little brandy? Not too sweet. I don't care for it, if it's too sweet. Something like Four-Star Hennessy or—

ELIZABETH. I'm sorry, Mrs. Smythe. But—

LOUISE. I'll get you something. Not brandy, but—no,

don't come with me! (*She goes to dining area to get* Tom's *bottle off table.*)

Mrs. Smythe. Has something happened?

Elizabeth. I'm afraid so, yes. To—Miss Beam. She—Mrs. Vickers tells me she was—stabbed.

Mrs. Smythe. She's—dead? (Elizabeth *nods.*) Oh, no! No! Why— I mean who?

Elizabeth. I know very little about it, Mrs. Smythe. Probably by the man you saw upstairs.

Mrs. Smythe. Oh. And to think I—I almost ran into him.

Louise. (*Comes back with a glass, in which she has poured some whiskey.*) Here. Be careful. It's straight. Do you more good.

Mrs. Smythe. Oh, thank you. I really need this. (*She takes a good sip.*) Very nice, Seagram's Seven, isn't it? (Louise *nods.*)

Elizabeth. (*Calling.*) Tom! Is that you?

Tom. (*In hall.*) Hello! Be with you in a minute.

Elizabeth. See anyone?

Tom. (*From off.*) No, but I heard the back door slam.

Mrs. Smythe. He's gone then. Oh, I'm so relieved.

Elizabeth. I wonder how he got in.

Louise. Do you lock up at night? Doors? Windows?

Elizabeth. Yes. We're very careful. Three months ago there was a burglary. Just down the road—at a place called Rollo's Tavern. Since then—

Louise. You do it yourself?

Elizabeth. Yes, or my brother when he— I mean, I always check, though.

Louise. Did you tonight?

Elizabeth. Why, I—no, I don't believe I did. I'm afraid I— Perhaps I'd better look now—and see if— (Elizabeth *goes to window Right.*) The catch is off. But that's always—I remember putting that catch on myself. Just before dinner. And I don't know why anyone should have opened it since then. (*As* Tom *appears in Right arch.*) Tom, we've found out how the— What's that?

TOM. (*Has a shawl in his hand.*) I went by your room and got this. Afraid you'd be cold.

ELIZABETH. (*Puzzled; she has on a good thick quilted bathrobe.*) Sweet of you, dear— But I didn't need it.

TOM. Oh. I didn't know. (*He tosses shawl on chair.*)

LOUISE. (*Hasn't missed this.*) Find the knife, Mr. Byron?

TOM. (*Momentarily startled.*) Knife?

MRS. SMYTHE. (*Her eyes wide.*) Knife? Oh, dear, you don't mean the knife that—that—that—

LOUISE. (*Nods towards the drink.*) Finish it. There's more where that came from! (MRS. SMYTHE *does finish it.*)

TOM. I wasn't looking for the knife, Mrs. Vickers.

LOUISE. Oh? You were a while ago. I thought maybe you might have stumbled on it—upstairs or downstairs—

MRS. SMYTHE. "Or in my lady's chamber." (*She giggles.*) Oh! I didn't mean to do that! It must be—nervous reaction.

LOUISE. (*Takes empty glass from her.*) Yes! Reaction.

ELIZABETH. We've found out how he got in, Tom. This window here. The catch is off. I forgot it; I guess you did too.

TOM. (*Going to window.*) I see.

ELIZABETH. I suppose Miss Beam heard him and—

MRS. SMYTHE. Oh, how horrible! All my life I've been afraid of burglars.

LOUISE. Burglars?

MRS. SMYTHE. Why, yes.

LOUISE. Oh, yes. Yes. Burglars.

TOM. (*Looks at her quickly.*) That must have been how it happened, don't you think, Mrs. Vickers? He came in the window, started along the hall. Miss Beam heard him—he picked up the knife—stabbed her—

LOUISE. And got out the back door?

TOM. Well—

LOUISE. Of course he wouldn't know exactly where the back door was—so he went upstairs looking for it.

Tom. I didn't mean quite that.

Elizabeth. You don't think it was a burglar, Mrs. Vickers?

Louise. I don't know, Miss Byron, I simply don't know.

Elizabeth. But it could have been.

Mrs. Smythe. Of course. And the reason he went upstairs was to steal something.

Louise. Steal what?

Mrs. Smythe. Goodness. I don't know. But I—I can't believe a burglar would break into a house—and not take a little something.

Louise. No. At least a cup and saucer, a pair of earrings for his little girl.

Elizabeth. I don't believe I quite understand, Mrs. Vickers.

Louise. I'm sorry. It just seems so odd that at last I'm going to make the acquaintance of my old friend—the well-known tramp.

Mrs. Smythe. You have a friend—who's a *tramp?*

Louise. Not quite. I take it you don't read mystery stories.

Mrs. Smythe. Oh, I wouldn't read one of those things for anything in the world.

Louise. If you did you'd— In almost every one I ever heard of—at some time or other—there's talk of an outsider—someone who is just strolling by—enters the living-room window—murders somebody just for the fun of it—and goes on his merry way.

Mrs. Smythe. Oh, I think that's awful.

Louise. So do I.

Tom. (*Smiles slightly.*) I know what you mean, of course, Mrs. Vickers—but still—

Louise. You're right! Mr. Byron. "But still," there's always a first time. So we must find out what's missing. How about you, Mrs. Smythe?

Mrs. Smythe. Oh, no! I have a little trick. It's one my dear husband taught me. He travelled a lot and when he was going away he'd say, "Put all your jewelry under your pillow, Blossom. Then if they want to rob you, they'll have to kill you first."

LOUISE. I'm just the opposite. I spread everything I own on top of the dresser where nobody could possibly miss it. Then I crawl into bed with a "Do Not Disturb" sign around my neck.

ELIZABETH. Mrs. Vickers, even if nothing is missing, the man could have gone upstairs *to* steal something, couldn't he? Then when Mrs. Smythe saw him he'd realize her scream would wake up the household so he—

LOUISE. Say that again, will you?

ELIZABETH. What?

LOUISE. What you just said.

ELIZABETH. I said he went upstairs *to* steal—

LOUISE. No. No. "He knew Mrs. Smythe's scream would wake up the household." But it didn't, did it!

ELIZABETH. What are you talking about?

LOUISE. I'm slipping. I'm slipping badly. . . . Her scream *didn't* wake up the household. The only person it woke up was *you*. Your brother and I were already up. Why didn't it wake up the others? Mrs. Walker?

ELIZABETH. She had a sleeping pill, remember?

LOUISE. A very mild one.

TOM. Yes, but—well, after Mrs. Smythe came down to get you, I went by and gave Corinne a good shot of hooch.

ELIZABETH. Oh, Tom!

LOUISE. Hooch and sleeping pills don't mix.

TOM. I didn't know about the sleeping pill, and you see when I called up Fred tonight— (*Explains to* LOUISE.) Fred's her husband—to say Corinne was staying here, he told me since her breakdown she'd taken to walking in her sleep.

ELIZABETH. Oh, no!

TOM. He said he always gave her a good strong hot toddy at bedtime to relax her.

LOUISE. But the maid, Martha—if that's her name?

ELIZABETH. Her room is way in the back.

LOUISE. The cook.
ELIZABETH. Her room's back there, too.
TOM. Besides she's very deaf.
LOUISE. Your aunt, then, Mrs.—
ELIZABETH. Aunt Laura drinks her ovaltine—and she's good till six in the morning.
LOUISE. But the nurse? Nurses are usually light sleepers. They usually keep one ear open— (*She stops. Slowly.*) unless. . . . My God!
ELIZABETH. What is it?
MRS. SMYTHE. Oh, dear. Now what? Something horrible?
LOUISE. Something Harriet said.
TOM. What, Mrs. Vickers?
LOUISE. No, please. (*She sees the empty glass in* MRS. SMYTHE'S *hand.*) You'd like some more of this perhaps?
MRS. SMYTHE. Well, it— (*She giggles.*) it does help.
LOUISE. Maybe it will help me, too. (*She starts for dining area but stops, as the DOORBELL rings.*)
ELIZABETH. The police, I imagine!
LOUISE. The police?
ELIZABETH. Yes.
LOUISE. I don't think so. Not unless they're psychic.
TOM. I haven't called the police.
MRS. SMYTHE. You haven't called the—?
TOM. (*Quickly.*) There wasn't time, was there, Mrs. Vickers? (*To* MRS. SMYTHE.) She and I found the body—almost immediately after we heard you scream. So there wasn't time. Isn't that right, Mrs. Vickers? You—agree, don't you, Mrs. Vickers? (*He looks at her. It's as though he said, "Will you keep the bargain?"*)
LOUISE. (*Gets his meaning.*) Yes, Mr. Byron, I agree.

(ELIZABETH *is puzzled.* TOM *goes out into hall.* LOUISE *goes to dining area, ostensibly to get* MRS. SMYTHE *a drink. But as soon as she turns the corner and is out of sight of* ELIZABETH, *she sets down the glass, and with a quick glance at the covered body, she hurries out through the swinging door.)*

TOM. (*Offstage.*) Ronnie!
RONNIE. (*Offstage.*) Sorry to wake you up, Tom, but I've got to see Aunt Laura.
TOM. We are up. (*The two men are seen at Right archway.*)
RONNIE. Oh, hello, Liz. That's all right then. Glad I didn't wake you. I'll just—
ELIZABETH. No, wait! You know very well, Ronnie, you can't disturb Aunt Laura this time of night.
RONNIE. I've got to, Liz. This is an emergency. Mother's—taken a turn for the worse. I've got to see her and—
MRS. SMYTHE. And get a check? (*She giggles.*)
RONNIE. Who the hell is she?
ELIZABETH. Mrs. Smythe.
RONNIE. Oh, yes. She's the one—
MRS. SMYTHE. Oh. We've met but you weren't very nice. (*Another giggle.*) Mrs. Gensett says she doesn't think your mother's as shick as you say she is.
RONNIE. What are you talking about?
MRS. SMYTHE. She says if you'd stop tinkerling the—tick-er-ling the keys. (*A giggle.*) Oh, that's funny isn't it? "Tickerling the keys"—and went to work—
RONNIE. You're crazy! (*He starts off.*)
TOM. Just a minute, Ronnie.
RONNIE. Sorry, I'm in a hurry.
TOM. (*Blocks him.*) Oh, no.
RONNIE. Say, what the hell is this? All right—all right, I want a check. I've got to have it. Why shouldn't I have it?
TOM. We're not talking about a check.
RONNIE. Like hell. You stopped her from giving it to me before—
TOM. I did what?
RONNIE. You or Elizabeth—or somebody.

ELIZABETH. Then it was somebody.

RONNIE. (*To* MRS. SMYTHE.) Or maybe it was *you*. Yeah, it could have been you. Please, Tom, I've got to see Aunt—

TOM. We're not talking about a check. There's been some trouble here tonight.

RONNIE. Oh, what—sort of trouble?

TOM. For one thing, a burglar—and—

MRS. SMYTHE. (*Suddenly pointing at* RONNIE.) Ooooo! I bet it was him!

TOM. What?

MRS. SMYTHE. "He."

RONNIE. "He"— "Him"— What is she—?

MRS. SMYTHE. The man upstairs! The burglar. He was wearing a coat then but—

ELIZABETH. Where is your coat, Ronnie? You were wearing it before.

RONNIE. I left it in the car.

ELIZABETH. Why?

RONNIE. Hell! I don't know why, I just did.

ELIZABETH. (*Moves towards window.*) Strange. I didn't hear you drive up and that car of yours makes quite a lot of noise.

RONNIE. I didn't drive up. I left the car down by the gate. (*As she looks at him.*) Because it *does* make a lot of noise, I didn't want to wake everybody up.

ELIZABETH. But you rang the doorbell. That would wake—

RONNIE. I had to get in, didn't I? The bell rings near you. I thought you'd let me in quietly. I could see Aunt Laura and— God, I didn't think I'd have to go through all this. Questions, suspicions—are you satisfied? Because if you are, I'd like to see Aunt Laura.

ELIZABETH. She won't like being disturbed.

RONNIE. I wouldn't have to disturb her if all of you didn't build such a wall around her.

TOM. What's that?

RONNIE. Yes. You and Elizabeth and Corinne—Cousin

George—the whole damn lot of you. You've been trying to freeze me out. (*Turns to* Mrs. Smythe.) And you, too, I expect. Well, I'm not going to be freezed out. And I'm warning you, Tom—if you try to stop me—I'm going to turn nasty. So—

(*As he turns to archway,* Louise *appears there and holds out a cigarette lighter.*)

Louise. Is this yours?
Ronnie. Oh, yes. Thanks. Where—?
Louise. In Mrs. Gensett's room.
Ronnie. Oh, yeah. I—I must have dropped it in there —when I was here before.
Tom. Wait a minute! You said the nurse wouldn't let you in before.
Ronnie. She didn't "let me," but I slipped by. I spoke to Aunt Laura—asked if I could come back—she said I could—
Elizabeth. I don't believe you, Ronnie.
Ronnie. All right. Ask her! *Ask her!*
Louise. You're quite safe in saying that, aren't you?
Tom. Why do you say that, Mrs. Vickers?
Louise. Mrs. Gensett is lying on the floor—just inside her room. From the expression on her face—I'd say she'd been . . . frightened to death.
Mrs. Smythe. (*After a pause.*) No, no! Oh, no! Mrs. Gensett! Poor, dear Mrs.— Oh, no. (*Suddenly turns on* Ronnie.) And you did it! He did it! He killed her! He *was* the man I saw upstairs!
Louise. Please, Mrs. Smythe!
Mrs. Smythe. He did! He did! He killed her! And I bet he'd just come from there when I saw—
Louise. Quiet! There's something else. (*To* Tom.) I found the knife.
Ronnie. Knife? What knife?
Tom. Where?
Louise. At the top of the stairs there's some curtains. I don't know what's behind them.

ELIZABETH. Nothing really. An alcove. My mother used it as a sewing-room.

LOUISE. At the bottom of the curtains. The knife was there. There's blood on it.

MRS. SMYTHE. Oh, my God! Don't! I can't stand things like that. I'm going to be sick. I'm going to be—

LOUISE. All right—all right. Go somewhere and be sick. In a minute I'll be along myself, only— (*Sharply.*) Where are you going, Mr. Byron?

TOM. Upstairs. Why?

LOUISE. It isn't necessary.

TOM. I don't know what you mean by that, but Aunt Laura, are you sure she's—?

LOUISE. Quite sure.

TOM. You won't mind if I make sure myself, will you?

LOUISE. I can't very well stop you, can I? But I'm warning you, don't touch anything. Especially don't touch that knife.

TOM. I had no intention of doing so, Mrs. Vickers. (*He goes.*)

RONNIE. Say, what is this? What is this?

ELIZABETH. Yes, Mrs. Vickers, what did that mean?

LOUISE. I think I prefer your asking your brother. Let him explain.

RONNIE. I don't get this. What's this about a knife?

LOUISE. Sorry. And now, Miss Byron, will you call the police or shall I?

ELIZABETH. I'll call them, Mrs. Vickers. (*She starts for hall.*)

LOUISE. I'll make some black coffee for the nurse.

ELIZABETH. What's that?

LOUISE. The nurse has been drugged; at least I can't wake her up. (*She starts for dining room area, suddenly stops.*)

ELIZABETH. You say the nurse—

(LOUISE *waves her hand for silence.*)

MRS. SMYTHE. (*In a loud whisper.*) Oh. What is it? What is it?

LOUISE. (*In a low voice.*) That—swinging door is swinging.

MRS. SMYTHE. That's what a swinging door is supposed to do, isn't it? (*She giggles. The giggle is followed by a hiccup.*)

RONNIE. (*To* MRS. SMYTHE.) Why don't you sober up?

MRS. SMYTHE. Don't you talk to me like that—you—you murderer.

LOUISE. Please!

RONNIE. (*Goes to* LOUISE.) You mean somebody was out there? (LOUISE *nods.*) Shall I go see who—?

LOUISE. Too late now. Better stay here. Miss Byron—please—call the police.

(LOUISE *goes towards swinging door, and slowly* ELIZABETH *goes into hall, to telephone.* RONNIE *turns back towards* MRS. SMYTHE.)

MRS. SMYTHE. (*Backs away from* RONNIE.) Well—I'm certainly not going to stay here. Just with you. (*She hurries out Right archway.*)

ELIZABETH. (*Her voice heard in hall.*) Operator . . . operator. (*There is a piercing scream from* MRS. SMYTHE. *A noise as* ELIZABETH *evidently drops the telephone receiver.* LOUISE, *at swinging door, stops, then hurries back into living room.* MRS. SMYTHE *returns running, as if all the devils of hell were after her.*) What is it? What—Corinne!

RONNIE. Great God! Lady Macbeth!

(*From the darkened hall a strange apparition appears.* CORINNE *is wearing a borrowed negligee of* ELIZABETH'S, *which is too long for her. Her hair is wild and flowing. Her eyes are glazed and she totters.* ELIZABETH *rushes to hold her.* CORINNE'S *body sways.*)

ACT II   A HOME FOR STRAY CATS   63

ELIZABETH. Ronnie! Ronnie! (RONNIE *goes to* CORINNE'S *other side to help support her.*) Are you hurt? Corinne! Corinne!

RONNIE. I don't think so.

ELIZABETH. Get her in a chair.

MRS. SMYTHE. (*Crosses to* LOUISE.) Oh! I just can't take these things.

LOUISE. What things?

MRS. SMYTHE. Being frightened to death. Every five minutes. It's not good for me.

LOUISE. I don't care for it either.

MRS. SMYTHE. I need—where the—you know?

LOUISE. There! (*Points to liquor bottle on table.* MRS. SMYTHE *starts.*) Don't trip over the body.

MRS. SMYTHE. (*Stops.*) The— Oh, no! No! Please, I—you—you'll have to get it for me!

LOUISE. All right. (*Goes quickly to table, gets bottle and gives it to* MRS. SMYTHE.) Better sit down to it. You won't have so far to fall. (LOUISE *gives her a gentle shove into chair, Center.* ELIZABETH *and* RONNIE *have got* CORINNE *into large chair, Right.*) Is she all right?

ELIZABETH. Seems to be.

LOUISE. Can she talk?

RONNIE. (*Gets a whiff of her breath.*) If you ask me she's drunk as a hoot owl. (*He rises.*)

LOUISE. Another one. (*Looks over at* MRS. SMYTHE, *then to* RONNIE.) Can you make coffee? (*He nods.*) Go make some then. Strong and black.

RONNIE. (*He starts for dining area. Suddenly stops.*) What—what's that? (*Points at covered figure on the floor.*)

LOUISE. My secretary.

RONNIE. What—she's dead?

MRS. SMYTHE. She's dead. Mrs. Gensett's dead. Everybody's dead! Poor, dear Mrs. Gensett!

LOUISE. A crying jag. That's all we need. (RONNIE *goes through swinging door.* LOUISE *turns to* ELIZABETH.) The police. Did you call them?

ELIZABETH. I started to when—

LOUISE. Please do it now, will you?

ELIZABETH. Of course. (*She takes a few steps; stops.*) Mrs. Vickers, why were you warning my brother about touching the knife?

LOUISE. You don't know?

ELIZABETH. If I knew I wouldn't ask.

LOUISE. Ever since we discovered Harriet's body, your brother has been trying to find the knife. He went out in the hall looking for it. When Mrs. Smythe saw the burglar and he went up, I'm pretty certain he was looking for it. When I announced I'd found your aunt's body, he didn't make a move. But when I said I'd found the knife, he immediately went up again. I think he wants to wipe off the handle.

ELIZABETH. But why? Oh, you don't think he used the knife, do you?

LOUISE. If he had, he'd have wiped it off a long time ago. He even went in *your* room—using that shawl there as an excuse for going there. (*She turns to look at* MRS. SMYTHE.)

ELIZABETH. I see. Meaning he thought I used it.

LOUISE. I have no right to question you— Wait! Out like a light! (*She removes bottle from* MRS. SMYTHE'S *hands.*)

ELIZABETH. I—I don't mind being questioned—in the least. (*But she begins to twist the handkerchief in her hands.*)

LOUISE. Did you know Harriet Beam before she came here? Did you know who she was? Had you ever heard of her?

ELIZABETH. No. I—I— (*Her lips tremble. Suddenly she breaks.*) Oh, my God! I— No. I didn't know her but—but—I knew there was a woman in New York—that my brother had an affair with. I didn't know who she was until—when Miss Beam arrived I—I—

LOUISE. Your brother told you?

ELIZABETH. No, no! But when they met—the way they

acted—the things they said—the things they didn't say. I—I can't explain, but I knew.

LOUISE. (*Kindly.*) You and your brother are very close?

ELIZABETH. Yes. I'm two years older. Our father died when we were very young. My mother—Aunt Laura's younger sister—tried to raise us but she—she—she wasn't —well. She had a mental breakdown and—she died in a rest home. Tom went to New York. I had a job in Hartford for a while, but I—I lost it. We tried to sell this house. But nobody wanted it. Too big. So I—I finally came back and—and—

LOUISE. I'm very sorry. I shouldn't have put you through this, but perhaps it's just as well. You'd better be prepared when the police get here.

ELIZABETH. Yes, yes, the police. I was about to call them, wasn't I? (*She goes just out of sight, to telephone table.*) Hello. . . . Hello. . . . Operator—operator. . . . The phone is dead.

LOUISE. (*Hurrying to Right arch.*) Give it to me! (*In Right arch we see her take the receiver; she pulls at cord, and we see the end of it.*) The wire's been cut.

ELIZABETH. Oh, with these. (*She appears in archway, holding a pair of gardening shears. They are the old-fashioned kind, meant to be used with one hand, and with very sharp points at the end.*) They were on the table here.

LOUISE. I see. You shouldn't have touched them, but I don't suppose it matters. Put them back please. (ELIZABETH *leans over to do so.*) Before when you tried to use the phone. Was it dead then?

ELIZABETH. I don't know. Mrs. Smythe screamed just then, so I—

LOUISE. Probably cut some time ago. Where are those shears kept?

ELIZABETH. On top of an old chest in the back hall. Just outside the door to the kitchen. Along with a trowel, a weed-killer—the usual things.

LOUISE. So anybody could have picked them up. Miss Byron, something that's been bothering me. Your maid, Martha—if that's her name. Have you had her long?

ELIZABETH. No. Two days. You mean her name isn't Martha?

LOUISE. I don't think so. Where did you get her? An agency? An ad in papers?

ELIZABETH. No. As a matter of fact, I had a phone call from her. She said she heard I needed a maid. A little later she arrived—in a taxi—from Bridgeport.

LOUISE. You didn't check on her? References or anything?

ELIZABETH. I'm afraid not. I was too glad to have her. It's difficult to get anybody way out here. What about her, Mrs. Vickers?

LOUISE. One or two things have puzzled me, and a while ago—when that swinging door was swinging—I thought I caught a glimpse of her uniform.

(TOM *appears at Right arch.*)

ELIZABETH. Tom, the telephone wire's been cut.

TOM. Oh?

LOUISE. I expect he knows that.

TOM. What does that mean, Mrs. Vickers?

LOUISE. *You* cut the wire, Mr. Byron.

TOM. Why would I do that?

LOUISE. To delay calling the police until you could get hold of that knife and wipe the prints off it.

TOM. Oh, now. Just a minute!

LOUISE. Now, I think you've done that so—

ELIZABETH. Oh, Tom, you thought I killed Miss Beam.

TOM. Of course not. Why would you want to—?

LOUISE. It's no use, Mr. Byron. Your sister knows about you and Harriet. No, I didn't tell her. She guessed.

TOM. But how—? I mean—even so, she'd have no motive for—

LOUISE. Yes. She'd have a good motive. She may have thought Harriet was here to take you away from her.

ELIZABETH. (*In a strange tone.*) Maybe—I did.
TOM. What?
ELIZABETH. Maybe I did kill her.
TOM. Don't say that!
ELIZABETH. No. Let's face it. When I was working in Hartford I had a blackout. I wrote you about it. I blanked out for several hours. (*She sinks in a chair.*)
TOM. (*Goes to kneel before her.*) No, you couldn't have! It's impossible, you just couldn't have! Put that idea right out of your mind! When the police get here—

(*He is interrupted by the loud ringing of the DOORBELL.*)

LOUISE. Now what? Would you like me to go? (ELIZABETH *nods.* LOUISE *goes through Right arch and disappears, Off Right.* LOUISE's *voice is heard, as she evidently opens the DOOR.*) Yes?
MAN'S VOICE. (*Off Right.*) State Police, I understand you've had a little trouble here.
LOUISE. (*Off Right.*) The understatement of the year! May I ask how you found out about it? Our phone isn't working.
MAN'S VOICE. Had a call from Rollo's Tavern, a woman. I've sent a man to pick her up. (LOUISE *appears in archway Right and therefore is now in the light.*) Say, I know you, don't I? Wait! I've got it! Louise Vickers! You write about murder, don't you?
LOUISE. (*Nods.*) I did! But now I think I'll write about the "Birds and the Bees"— (*She smiles, looking at him.*) Not as exciting as murder. Or is it! I've forgotten.

CURTAIN

ACT THREE

TIME: *Half an hour later. The scene is the same except that Harriet's body has been removed.*

AT RISE: LOUISE *is seated at extreme Right.* LIEUTENANT SCOTT, *of the Connecticut State Police, is standing in Right archway, looking at the piece of yellow paper which* LOUISE *extracted from the typewriter in the previous scene.* SCOTT *is in the late thirties.*

SCOTT. She certainly didn't mince words about these people. Seems to have had a down on everybody in the house. You say you found this in the typewriter, and took it out after you found her body?
LOUISE. Yes. When Tom Byron went upstairs in answer to Mrs. Smythe's scream. He knew about that yellow paper. And asked me about it. I lied—said I didn't have it.
SCOTT. Why?
LOUISE. I like the people in this house—or most of them. I'm old-fashioned, I guess. I didn't want them to see it and get their feelings hurt.
SCOTT. Why are you showing it to me now?
LOUISE. Because Tom Byron thought I was jealous of Harriet. Also, you know what a gimmick is?
SCOTT. Sure. It's a twist—or something—at the end of a story. Is that right?
LOUISE. Right. Harriet decided to write a story, using the people here as characters. She figured that practically all of them were anxious to kill the old lady, Mrs. Gensett, to get the inheritance.
SCOTT. Well, where's the gimmick?
LOUISE. At the bottom of the page there.
SCOTT. (*Reading.*) "Reverse it. Have the victim the murderer." I don't believe I get that.

Louise. I'm not sure I do either. What I *think* she means though is that instead of having one or more of the potential heirs kill the old lady, she was going to have the old lady kill them.

Scott. But that's not the way it happened, is it?

Louise. No.

Scott. Unless—suppose Miss Beam's gimmick happened to be right. I mean suppose the old lady came downstairs—killed Miss Beam—then went upstairs and had a heart attack.

Louise. But why would she kill Harriet?

Scott. By mistake. Thinking she was someone else. Or maybe— Forget the motive for the moment. Just think of the sequence. (Louise *shakes her head*.) You don't think much of that idea, do you?

Louise. Frankly, no. You see I'm trying to be fair.

Scott. Fair?

Louise. I'll explain that later. What you suggest would be a nice idea—a really *lovely* idea. It would get everybody off the hook—all the people in the house. The killer kills—then dies herself—in just retribution. All very nice —and *pat*. It's like the other idea suggested tonight—the tramp who comes sauntering in, commits a murder, and then saunters away. That too was a nice idea. That too would let everybody off the hook—myself included. But my intelligence wouldn't let me accept it.

Scott. I see. Now—what did you mean by being fair?

Louise. (*Smiles*.) Oh, that. It's rather difficult to—to express, but—well, despite the horror of the things that have happened tonight—Harriet's death—and all that— at odd moments I get the—the feeling that they are not *really* happening—that I'm making them up—that it's a *story* I'm writing.

Scott. You mean you—you're objective about it?

Louise. Something like that. And being a mystery writer, I feel I have to—to adhere to the code—*my* code —not to cheat. I don't know if I'm getting through to you, but—

SCOTT. I think I see what you're driving at. Hm. The medical examiner says the old lady's death was due to a heart attack. That, of course, doesn't mean very much since most people die of heart attacks. He can't tell whether it was—well, just accidental or whether it was brought about deliberately. (*Looks down at paper again.*) Well, from this we know what Miss Beam thought of the people in the house. What do *you* think of them?

LOUISE. I don't really know them, Lieutenant.

SCOTT. You're a very clever woman, Mrs. Vickers. Obviously an observant one. I'd like your opinion on this. You say you liked them?

LOUISE. I said I liked *some* of them.

SCOTT. Which ones?

LOUISE. Please, Lieutenant. I'm not really prepared to—to—say, I mean—well, let's put it this way. I—I felt sorry for them.

SCOTT. Sorry for them?

LOUISE. Yes. That old woman—enormously wealthy—must have been a fiend out of hell. She played with them—like a cat with mice. She dangled her money in front of them—then took it out of their sight. She made wills—tore them up. Promised them checks—then didn't come through. From what I've heard, she seemed to enjoy this situation—using her power to torture people. If one of them had—well, grabbed a knife and stabbed her, I could have—understood it.

SCOTT. Instead of which, one of them grabbed a knife and stabbed your secretary. So—we get back to the death of your secretary.

LOUISE. Yes, we always get back to that.

SCOTT. Which means we have to find someone who had a motive for killing her. When I first arrived Miss Elizabeth Byron asked to speak to me privately. She said she knew her brother had had an affair with Miss Beam. And she admitted to me she had once blanked out while working in Hartford. Personally I've had no experience with a case of murder committed by a person who had blanked out, but I've heard of them. I should think it would come pretty close to a kind of—well, temporary insanity. So Elizabeth Byron is a prime suspect. Then there's her brother—

LOUISE. Wait! If he thought his sister did it, that would mean he couldn't have done it himself.

SCOTT. Not necessarily. Knowing his sister was innocent, he might have used that as a blind—hoping we'd think just what you're thinking now.

LOUISE. Y-yes. I see that. But why would Tom kill her? They had broken up. She didn't want him back. She told me so. And he didn't want her. So why would he want to kill her?

SCOTT. Something we don't know about.

LOUISE. Such as?

SCOTT. (*Shrugs.*) I wouldn't know. But love can cause a lot of trouble.

LOUISE. But they weren't in love any longer.

SCOTT. Well, when people fall out of love there're sometimes a lot of hangovers. And speaking of that, Tom Byron is an alcoholic. He's the only member of the family I ever had any dealings with. We pinched him for driving under the influence. Took his license away. Gosh! I wish somebody from the sheriff's office would get here and take over.

LOUISE. Sheriff's office?

SCOTT. Yes. It's their baby. Of course we work with 'em, but—trouble is the sheriff himself is in Hartford attending the Governor's Law Enforcement Conference—and his chief deputy's in the hospital with a bullet wound in his leg. Oh, they'll send somebody, but meantime—well, it's up to me. Look, Mrs. Vickers. Somebody once said that the clue to a murderer could generally be found in the personality of the victim. You've told me a little about Miss Beam. Tell me a little more. You say she tricked you into coming here?

LOUISE. Yes.

SCOTT. And you resented it.

LOUISE. I did indeed. I resented it very much. (*A slight pause.* LOUISE *smiles.*) Aren't you going to ask me if I resented it enough to kill her?

SCOTT. All right, I'll ask you.

LOUISE. No.

SCOTT. Hm. Seems to me if you wanted to get rid of her, you wouldn't have to kill her. You could just fire her.

LOUISE. I did.

SCOTT. When?

LOUISE. Tonight.

SCOTT. Because she tricked you into coming here?

LOUISE. Partially that. And partially because she'd left that paper in the typewriter. She went off—to make a plan of the house, she said. Anyone could have gone in the dining room and seen that paper. Not knowing that Harriet was writing on her own, they'd have thought I had dictated it to her.

SCOTT. A plan of the house, hm. We found one—I guess it was hers. It's a crazy sort of house. Do you think she might have met someone while she was going through it—? Or maybe stumbled on something, say, that would make her a danger to someone?

LOUISE. That I don't know.

SCOTT. Where were you?

LOUISE. Upstairs. Mrs. Gensett had sent for me. For what reason I don't know, as I never saw her. It was then I saw the photograph. I went to my own room then—to sort of think things over.

SCOTT. Besides you and Tom Byron, could Miss Beam have known any of these people before she came here. In New York, say?

LOUISE. If she did, that fact never came out. And I rather doubt it. Mrs. Walker is—well— (*She smiles.*) She has four children—and makes rather a point of it. Also, I gather she is hard up. I doubt if she got to New York much.

SCOTT. Mrs.—er—the one who'd passed out drunk?

LOUISE. Smythe? If she and Harriet had ever met before, they didn't say so. Harriet thought she was pretty much of a phony—and I'm inclined to agree.

SCOTT. Phony? In what way?

LOUISE. Oh, too good to be true. . . . Sweet! And coy! And kittenish! Besides being a horrible bore. Mrs. Walker and she had a terrible scene—at least Mrs. Walker made the scene. Accused the other woman of latching on to the old lady to get money out of her. It was pretty ghastly.

SCOTT. Hm. What about the nurse?

LOUISE. The nurse. I don't know. She's an unknown quantity, as far as I'm concerned. She— Wait a minute! I just remembered. Something I heard—or overheard—or—well, heard without hearing if you know what I mean.

SCOTT. I'm afraid I don't.

LOUISE. I was at the dining room table. Making some notes. And I sort of heard a conversation between Elizabeth Byron and that young man—er—Ronnie Bliss. Something about the nurse being a—well, a spy. For another member of the family. The family calls him Cousin George.

SCOTT. So—well, what about young Bliss? He's a musician—they usually get around a lot. Do you suppose he might have known Miss Beam in New York?

LOUISE. I shouldn't think so, but then— I don't know.

SCOTT. I want to talk to that young man anyway, so—

(TOM *comes through swinging door, and moves directly Downstage. He speaks to* SCOTT.)

TOM. Do we have to wait around any longer? You told us to stay in the kitchen. But my sister is very tired. She's had an upsetting evening and—

SCOTT. That's all right, Mr. Byron. I asked you to stay in there just while my men were searching the house.

(ELIZABETH *comes through the swinging door.* TOM *turns to her, and puts out his hand.*)

TOM. It's all right, Liz. You can go and lie down.

ELIZABETH. (*Moving Downstage.*) Thank you.
SCOTT. Are the others still in the kitchen?
ELIZABETH. Yes. Ronnie, my cousin, Mrs. Walker, and Mrs. Smythe. I made a large pot of coffee. If you'd like a cup, Mrs. Vickers—or you, Lieutenant, I can—

(SCOTT *shakes his head.*)

LOUISE. If I do, I'll get it myself.
TOM. No, no. I'll get it. (*To* ELIZABETH, *who has moved Upstage towards Right arch.*) Shall I come with you?
ELIZABETH. No, dear. I'll be all right. I want to get this robe off. I've torn the hem somehow, and I keep tripping. (*She goes through Right arch, and to back of hall.*)
SCOTT. (*To* TOM.) If you're going back to the kitchen, will you ask that young—er—Bliss to come in here?
TOM. Sure.
SCOTT. Just a minute. Do you have anything more you'd like to tell me, Mr. Byron?
TOM. Not that I know of. I've confessed to cutting the telephone wires—to wiping the prints off the knife. In other words I am what is known as an accessory after the fact. I don't believe I've any more crimes to my credit.
SCOTT. You did all that because you thought your sister might have killed Miss Beam.
TOM. I didn't say so, Lieutenant. (*He starts towards Left; then stops.*) Oh. Yours, I believe. I found it at the foot of the back stairs. (*He takes from his pocket the small black notebook—the one* LOUISE *was writing in in Act One, and hands it to her.*)
LOUISE. Thank you. (*As she takes the book, she sees* SCOTT *looking at it with curiosity. She smiles.*) Would you like to see this?

(TOM *has started towards dining area.*)

SCOTT. Is it something I *should* see?
LOUISE. I don't think so. But you're welcome.

ACT III A HOME FOR STRAY CATS

SCOTT. Well, since you offer it. (*He smiles, takes it, and starts thumbing through it.*)
TOM. (*Opens swinging door, and calls.*) Ronnie. The Lieutenant wants you. (*He does not exit; but stands near dining room table.*)
SCOTT. (*Still thumbing through the pages.*) Don't see much help here.
LOUISE. I didn't think you would.
SCOTT. Notes you write to yourself? I do that too sometimes. (*Turns another page.*) "Stern Brothers."
LOUISE. About a charge-o-plate.
SCOTT. My wife has an account there. (*Turns another page.*) "Nitro." What does that mean?
LOUISE. Nitroglycerin tablets. A reminder to send for more. My supply is running low.
SCOTT. Oh. You have a—heart condition? (*She nods.*) Serious?
LOUISE. I'm afraid so. Yes.
SCOTT. I'm sorry. Here. (*He hands her the notebook. TOM's reaction to the above few speeches is very strange. He jerks his head up suddenly, as though something had struck him very forcibly. Then, as though thinking deeply, he mechanically sits in a chair at table. As SCOTT turns back to LOUISE, the NURSE appears in Right archway. She looks sleepy-eyed and a bit groggy, but her speech is sharp and incisive. She wears a long, expensive-looking housecoat, not quite the garment one associates with a nurse who usually wears something simple and easy to slip on.*) Oh, Miss Green. Feeling better?
NURSE. Who's in charge here? You? (*He nods.*) There's a policeman upstairs. He refuses to allow me to see my patient. He said she was—dead?
SCOTT. (*He nods.*) Are you feeling better?

(RONNIE *enters by swinging door, but stays in dining area.*)

NURSE. What? Yes? I was drugged.

SCOTT. Yes. I think you were.

NURSE. But why? I mean, who—who—and what happened to my patient?

SCOTT. That's one of the things we're trying to find out. There are several things we're trying to find out. I'd like to question you, but I'd like you to be fully awake—have all your faculties. I suggest you go to the kitchen. There's black coffee there.

NURSE. But I don't understand. Why are the police here? And what happened to my patient? Oh! Does this mean that—that her death was not natural?

SCOTT. That's what we're trying to determine. Please, Miss Green. Get that coffee.

NURSE. Yes. Yes. (*She starts; then stops.*) Oh, if Mrs. Gensett is dead, then there's someone who should be notified at once. Mr. George Byron. He lives in Norwalk—and his telephone number is—

SCOTT. That's all been attended to.

NURSE. Oh. I see. Very well. (*She goes out into hall, and to Up Left.*)

LOUISE. (*Waits a few seconds; then smiles.*) Forgive me, Lieutenant—a rank amateur criticizing a professional, but—

SCOTT. Go ahead. (*And he too smiles.*) Sherlock Holmes was always cleverer than Scotland Yard.

LOUISE. Thank you. It seems to me that you might have got more out of Miss Green by questioning her *now*—while she was slightly groggy—than by waiting for her brain to clear.

SCOTT. Possible. But I was thinking of something else. Tell me, when you found the old lady's body, and tried to wake up the nurse, did you by any chance think she was shamming?

LOUISE. Shamming? Oh, you mean about being drugged? No. No. I didn't think so. I felt pretty sure she was really drugged. But— Wait! The question is *when* she was drugged.

SCOTT. I don't follow you.

ACT III   A HOME FOR STRAY CATS   77

LOUISE. I mean it would make quite a nice alibi, wouldn't it—after a murder was committed—perhaps *two* murders—to give yourself a strong drug and pretend you were out of the picture all the time.
SCOTT. Perhaps. But she didn't drug herself.
LOUISE. You're sure?
SCOTT. Dead sure. Where is that young fellow I sent for?

(*He turns towards Left;* RONNIE, *who has been listening, moves Downstage, and pretends he has just come in.*)

RONNIE. You wanted to see me?
SCOTT. Yes. I didn't finish talking to you. Remember? The medical examiner and the others arrived just then—so—I was asking you about a prescription we found in your pocket. For your mother. You got that prescription from the drug store today. It said so on the bottle. What time today? (*As* RONNIE *hesitates.*) Better tell the truth. I can check, you know.
RONNIE. Late this afternoon—or rather early this evening.
SCOTT. And where did you go after you left the drug store? Did you go home?
RONNIE. No.
SCOTT. You came here?
RONNIE. Yes.
SCOTT. Then perhaps you'll tell me how it happens that the bottle—the prescription reads "For Sleep"—was opened. The bottle was not quite full. (RONNIE *starts to speak; but falters.*) Miss Byron told me that she prepared a tray with ovaltine on it for Mrs. Gensett and the nurse. Did you pour a little of that medicine into the cup for the nurse? *Did you?*
RONNIE. Yes! All right. Yes! Yes! Yes, I did!
SCOTT. That's a pretty serious offense. Drugging people. Want to tell me why you did it?
RONNIE. Yes. I wanted to see my aunt—quietly—alone.

But whenever I tried to see her—at my cousin, Mrs. Walker's house when she was staying there—the nurse always interfered. I thought if I could get the nurse out of the way I could get a check—get my mother to the hospital. My aunt had told me that if I came back tonight—a little later—she'd talk to me. So I—

SCOTT. And later on *did* she talk to you?

RONNIE. No, because I ran into that crazy drunken woman, that Mrs.—er—

SCOTT. Smythe?

RONNIE. Yes. She started yelling—and screaming! God! You could hear her all the way to Bridgeport. I got rattled so I beat it down the back stairs and out the back door.

SCOTT. So you were here three times tonight.

RONNIE. Y-yes.

SCOTT. Tom Byron let you in the last time. Who let you in the first time?

RONNIE. Mrs. Walker.

SCOTT. And what about the second time? Who let you in then?

RONNIE. Nobody. I mean—the door was open and—

SCOTT. I don't think so. It's a spring lock—and it was locked when I got here.

RONNIE. I—I came in the window.

SCOTT. No. Miss Byron says she locked the window herself. Somebody must have *let* you in. So—

MARTHA. (*Has appeared at Right archway.*) Better tell the truth, Ronnie!

MAN'S VOICE. (*Off Right, by front door.*) Here she is, Lieutenant.

SCOTT. O.K., Bailey.

RONNIE. Anne! Where have you been? I've been looking everywhere for— (*He has started towards her.*)

SCOTT. Stay away from her, Bliss! (*He turns towards* MARTHA. MARTHA *is looking a bit haggard and disheveled. She is wearing a coat over her maid's uniform.*) What is your name?

MARTHA. My name is Anne Wellington.
SCOTT. But you were using the name of Martha Riggs and working here as a maid? (*She nods.*) You were the one who called the police?
RONNIE. (*Surprised.*) *You* called the police?
SCOTT. (*Sternly.*) Keep out of this, young man!
MARTHA. I had to, Ronnie! I was—
SCOTT. Don't talk to him! Talk to me!
MARTHA. I—I'm very tired. Could I—sit down?
SCOTT. Sure. (*She sits.*) You left here, went to Rollo's Tavern and called the police. What did you do after that?
MARTHA. I called a taxi.
SCOTT. But you didn't wait for it.
MARTHA. No, they said they couldn't send one for a while. I told them I'd start walking to meet the taxi. I didn't like waiting at the tavern. There were a lot of drunks there. One of them started to get fresh. Then a police car came along—and picked me up. I don't know how they knew me.
SCOTT. A description from the bartender. You got change to make the phone calls—you seemed upset—so he remembered you. Where were you going if you'd got the taxi?
MARTHA. Home. I didn't want to get mixed up in—in anything. I knew I'd done wrong—coming here under false pretenses—and all that.
RONNIE. Look, Lieutenant. Whatever she did—it was my fault—she did it for me.
SCOTT. No. Now get this straight. You're not responsible for *her* actions any more than she's responsible for yours.
RONNIE. But we're engaged.

(SCOTT *looks at* MARTHA, *who nods.*)

MARTHA. He and I've known each other since we were kids. His mother's very ill. I know that. I go to see her often. Ronnie hoped to get some money from Mrs. Gensett. But he was being squeezed out by other members of the family. He asked me to come up here and try to find out what was going on. I—I didn't know what I was letting myself in for.

SCOTT. What do you mean?

MARTHA. This house! It's so—so—it's a horrible old place. The ceilings are too high—there are too many hallways—not enough light. And the people! You come on them unexpectedly. They startle you. Like that secretary woman. The one who's dead.

SCOTT. Oh. You knew Miss Beam was dead? How did you know?

MARTHA. I opened the swinging door to the dining room. I saw something on the floor—covered up. I heard Ronnie talking to Mrs. Vickers there.

SCOTT. Tell me. You say Miss Beam startled you. Where did you meet Miss Beam?

MARTHA. I met her twice. Once on the back stairs—after I'd got Mrs. Walker to bed. And once coming out of the kitchen. We ran smack into each other.

SCOTT. What did she say to you?

MARTHA. Nothing. I said, "Excuse me." She just glared at me—as though it was my fault. And it wasn't. She was looking down at a paper she had.

SCOTT. Did you like Miss Beam?

MARTHA. No. I thought she was a horrible person. She was rude. I wasn't a servant, but she thought I was. She was nasty. I hate people who are nasty to servants.

SCOTT. You knew Miss Beam was dead. Did you know that Mrs. Gensett was dead?

MARTHA. (*Looks at* RONNIE.) Your Aunt Laura? She's—dead too? (*Then to* SCOTT.) No, I didn't know that. No, I— (*Suddenly a strange change comes over her.*) Oh, God! (*She rises.*)

SCOTT and RONNIE. What is it?

MARTHA. (*She is trembling.*) H-how was she killed?

RONNIE. What's the matter, Anne?

MARTHA. *How was she killed?* (*She goes over to* LOUISE, *seated at extreme Right.*) Do you know?

LOUISE. They think she was frightened to death. Why, dear?

MARTHA. Oh! Then I—I saw it!

LOUISE. You saw it?

MARTHA. Yes! Yes! I mean— No! No, I heard it!

SCOTT. You say you saw it! Now you say you—

LOUISE. Please, Lieutenant! Can't you see she's— (*Slips an arm around* MARTHA.) What did you see, dear? Or hear? Suppose you sit down here and— Take it easy, now. Try to control yourself. Take your time and try and tell us about it. (*She gets* MARTHA *into a chair; and sits beside her.*)

MARTHA. (*Speaks with difficulty.*) I saw a woman— going along the hall upstairs—she opened the door to the old lady's room—started in. I heard a sound—sort of gasp —as if someone was breathing hard. The woman started into the room—then suddenly backed out.

SCOTT. Go on!

MARTHA. She went down the hall—to that curtained alcove—where I went to turn out the light—

SCOTT. Turn out the light?

MARTHA. Yes. So Ronnie could slip upstairs.

RONNIE. I asked her to do it! It wasn't—

SCOTT. Keep out of this! After you let him in, I suppose.

MARTHA. Yes.

SCOTT. All right. Let's get back. The woman went to the alcove. What did she do there?

MARTHA. Nothing that I— Yes! Yes! She dropped something. Something shiny. I saw it when it hit the floor.

SCOTT. (*To* LOUISE.) The knife. (LOUISE *nods.*)

MARTHA. Knife?

SCOTT. Never mind! What else did you see—or hear?

MARTHA. I heard a sort of thump—or thud—from Mrs. Gensett's room—like something falling.

SCOTT. That—something. Could it have been—a body?

MARTHA. Y-yes. And there was a kind of clatter—or crash—

SCOTT. (*To* LOUISE.) She grabbed at some bottles on her dressing table. (*To* MARTHA.) Then what?

MARTHA. Nothing. I mean—I don't know. I—I knew there was something wrong—but I didn't know what. I got frightened—I came down the back stairs—went to my room and locked myself in. I stayed there for a long time. And I didn't come out until—well, I told you the other—about seeing the secretary's body. Then I went to the tavern. I ran. I ran all the way.

SCOTT. Now, Miss Wellington. Who was the woman you saw upstairs?

MARTHA. I—I don't know.

SCOTT. But you just said you saw her.

MARTHA. Yes, I did, but I—I couldn't see the woman really. The light was behind her. Just her shadow.

SCOTT. But you could tell *something* about her. Was she tall—short? Was she thin—or—

MARTHA. (*A bit hysterically*.) I don't know! I couldn't tell. There was something that— Oh! Wait! The light! That was it!

SCOTT. The light behind her?

MARTHA. Yes. And on the floor.

SCOTT. Light—on the floor?

MARTHA. Yes. The light fixtures in this house—some of them are old-fashioned. Upstairs—in the hall—there was a naked bulb. But somebody tonight—maybe the nurse—didn't like the glare. Someone had put up a home-made shade—cardboard, I guess—so the light shined down on the floor. I saw the shadow of the woman—and I could see the way she walked.

SCOTT. Do you think you could recognize—the way she walked?

MARTHA. Y-yes. I think so. I'm not sure but—y-yes, I—

SCOTT. Bliss! Go to the kitchen—and tell those women out there I want to see them. All of them. The nurse, Mrs. Walker, Mrs. Smythe—all of them.

RONNIE. (*A bit puzzled, but he obeys*.) Sure. (*He goes

to dining area, glances at TOM.) What's the matter with you?

TOM. (*Almost to himself.*) I'm not sure, but I think I've just been knocked down by a ten-ton truck.

RONNIE. That makes two of us. (*He goes out through swinging door.*)

SCOTT. Miss Wellington, I want you to sit there by Mrs. Vickers. Just sit quietly and don't say anything. Just see if you can identify any of these women by the way they walk. Understand?

MARTHA. Yes. Yes. But it wasn't the way she walked. It was—it was something else.

SCOTT. What was it then? You'd just said—

MARTHA. I don't know. I don't know!

SCOTT. We'll try it anyway. I'll talk to them—and you watch as they move around.

(*A pause.* TOM, *in dining area, has been staring at the portieres covering Left arch. He suddenly rises, darts through the portieres, and returns almost immediately. In his hand are the shears. He is standing there when the swinging door opens, and* MRS. SMYTHE *comes in. She sees* TOM *with the shears and gives vent to a blood-curdling scream.*)

TOM. What the hell?

SCOTT. (*Hurrying towards Left.*) What's the matter in here?

MRS. SMYTHE. (*Pointing at* TOM.) He's got a knife! He tried to kill me!

TOM. I wasn't even near her! I wasn't even—

SCOTT. What are you doing with the shears?

TOM. I was about to try an experiment.

SCOTT. Put them down!

TOM. You've already got my fingerprints from it. (*He tosses the shears on the table.*)

SCOTT. I know— I know! But I'll do the experimenting around here. Come with me, Mrs. Smythe.

(Mrs. Smythe *moves Downstage.* Tom *sits at table again.*)

Mrs. Smythe. Oh, I just can't take these things! My nerves! They're— You're from the police, aren't you? Miss Byron told me you were here. I guess I must have fainted.
Scott. Quite a faint, yes. Feeling better?
Mrs. Smythe. Yes. I mean if I could— Oh, Mrs. Vickers, you—you gave me something, remember? It seemed to help me. I wonder if you could—er—?
Louise. Sorry, Mrs. Smythe. I don't believe there is any more.
Mrs. Smythe. (*To* Scott.) Perhaps then I could go upstairs?

(Corinne *comes through swinging door; pauses a second to look at* Tom; *then comes Downstage.*)

Scott. In a moment, Mrs. Smythe. Right now I— (*A* Policeman *has appeared at Right arch.*) Finished upstairs, Elkins?
Elkins. Just about, sir.
Scott. Find anything interesting?
Elkins. Nothing that seems to mean much. I made a list. Here. What next?
Scott. (*As he glances at the paper.*) Radio the sheriff's office again. See what's doing.
Elkins. Right.
Scott. (*Still looking at the paper.*) Oh, this last little item. Where'd you find it?
Elkins. Room Seven. (*He exits Right.*)
Mrs. Smythe. That's my room! What did they find? I—I didn't have anything in my room that—that—
Scott. (*Holds up his hand for silence; then reads:*) "One empty—one half-filled bottle of Four-Star Hennessey Brandy."

CORINNE. I knew it! I knew it!

MRS. SMYTHE. That's medicine! I'm supposed to have it! The doctor told me!

CORINNE. Officer, Elizabeth says Aunt Laura was murdered. If she was, that woman did it!

SCOTT. Just a minute, Mrs. Walker.

MRS. SMYTHE. I didn't! I didn't! I loved Mrs. Gensett!

CORINNE. That woman, officer—ask around Bridgeport. Every rich woman—elderly, alone—that woman attaches herself to her. Meets them at libraries—tea-rooms—bus stops. Worms herself in—

MRS. SMYTHE. That's a lie!

CORINNE. There was a very wealthy woman in Bridgeport—a widow—Mrs. Sedgwick. She died rather mysteriously. They said it was ptomaine—but that woman there was in the house at the time and—

MRS. SMYTHE. That's a lie! Another lie!

SCOTT. Please! Just a minute! Both of you! Mrs. Walker, if Mrs. Smythe was trying to get money out of your aunt, why would she want to kill her?

CORINNE. How would I know? Maybe on account of the will. Aunt Laura was always changing her will. Maybe she'd made one with that woman's name in it. And she killed Aunt Laura before it could be changed again. That's your job to find out! Not mine! I—I want to go home. I have four children to look after. I want my husband to come and get me. I hate this house! I always did. Aunt Laura should have stayed with me! Please! Can't I go home? I'm not well.

SCOTT. Your husband has been notified. As soon as he comes—

MRS. SMYTHE. (*Suddenly very sweet.*) No. You're not well, are you?

CORINNE. What do you mean by that?

MRS. SMYTHE. Shall I tell them about your—illness? And about *why* poor dear Mrs. Gensett left your home to come here?

(*The* NURSE *has come in swinging door; moves Downstage.*)

CORINNE. She had words with Fred. (*To* SCOTT.) Fred is my husband.

MRS. SMYTHE. (*Still sweetly.*) Yes, because he defended you. (*Turns to* SCOTT.) Poor dear soul—she walks in her sleep. Did you know?

SCOTT. Yes, I did know.

MRS. SMYTHE. The other night—when Mrs. Gensett was staying with her—she was sleep-walking—one of her children—the oldest girl—followed her to the kitchen—woke her up suddenly—

CORINNE. (*Menacingly moves her fingers.*) Don't you say that!

MRS. SMYTHE. She picked up a skillet and tried to brain the little—

NURSE. You fool! You idiot.

(*Quick as a flash,* CORINNE *makes for* MRS. SMYTHE'S *throat.* MRS. SMYTHE *screams, tries to duck.*)

SCOTT. Miss Green! Quick!

(*The* NURSE *is closer to* CORINNE; *she grabs her from behind and pinions her arms from the rear.* MARTHA *screams.* LOUISE *lets out a sharp cry.* TOM *moves Downstage, to behind the* NURSE. CORINNE *sputters unintelligible words interspersed with* "Sneak," "Snake," *etc. It's all over in a few seconds.*)

TOM. Need help?

NURSE. I can handle her. Just open the door to the kitchen. (*To* SCOTT.) Have somebody bring my bag down from upstairs. (*To* CORINNE *soothingly.*) Quiet down, now! You're all right! Take it easy!

(CORINNE *is now gasping and sobbing, as the* NURSE

gets her to swinging door, which TOM *holds open for them.*)

SCOTT. (*Has gone out Right arch to hall; and calls up.*) Ferguson! Go to the nurse's room, get her medical bag, and take it to the kitchen. (*He returns to Right arch, wiping his brow.*) Whew! (MRS. SMYTHE *is rubbing her throat.*) Are you hurt?

MRS. SMYTHE. Not really. But she's very strong, isn't she? I believe crazy people usually are. Poor dear! Tragic, isn't it? I feel so sorry for her.

SCOTT. (*With not too much sarcasm.*) Yes. I'm sure you do.

MRS. SMYTHE. I thought I ought to tell you about it. My duty! Poor dear Mrs. Gensett was *so* upset. She told Mr. Walker he ought to have his wife locked up. But he told her to mind her own business. That's why she came here. May I—er—go to my room now?

SCOTT. Yes. Sure. Have one on me—while you're up there.

MRS. SMYTHE. (*For a second, she pretends not to understand. Then:*) Oh, you mean the— Oh, that's medicine—really and truly—medicine. (*She turns at Right arch.*) And speaking of medicine—the nurse—she called me a fool, but I'm not! I know something about *her*, too.

SCOTT. (*He looks as though he would like to be rid of* MRS. SMYTHE.) Oh? What?

MRS. SMYTHE. She's not a nurse. A real nurse. I mean a *registered* nurse.

SCOTT. How do you know?

(TOM *comes through swinging door.*)

MRS. SMYTHE. Oh, just from the way she did things—little things—around the sick room. I told Mrs. Gensett to-night. I told her she ought to call up the Nurses' Registry and check on her. Poor dear Mrs. Gensett! That was such a lovely book we were reading! And now—she won't ever know how it came out! (*She goes through Right arch, and to stairs.*)

Scott. Whew! Women! I don't mind a good old-fashioned *brawl*—in a bar-room! With fists flying—and clubs and knives—even guns! But when a couple of women bare their teeth—and show their claws—that's when I want to call it quits. I'd almost like to go back to my old job.

Louise. What was your old job, Lieutenant?

Scott. Arresting speeders and picking up mangled corpses from the Merritt Parkway. (Ronnie *comes through swinging door, moves Downstage.*) Now, Miss Wellington! Notice anything about any of those three women?

Martha. (*Rises.*) No. No, I didn't.

Scott. Not the way one of them walked—or the way—?

Martha. It wasn't the way she walked. It—

Scott. You said it was.

Martha. I know. But it wasn't just that!

Scott. What was it then? *What was it?*

Martha. I don't know! I don't know! I don't know! Oh, Ronnie! (*She runs to him; he puts his arms around her.*)

Ronnie. (*Angrily.*) Look here, Lieutenant! You've got no right to—

Scott. All right—all right—all right! She doesn't know. Take her out to the kitchen—soothe her down—give her some coffee—or get the nurse to give her a tranquilizer—or something. (Ronnie *and* Martha *start Upstage.*) But, listen; both of you! (*They turn back. As they do,* Elizabeth *appears in Right arch. She is wearing the dress she wore at the beginning of the play.*) I don't want you to leave yet. Any of you! Understand! I want you on hand to— What is it, Miss Wellington?

Martha. (*Has raised her hand, and is pointing at* Elizabeth.) She—she's the one!

Scott. What's that?

MARTHA. She's the one I saw upstairs!
TOM. Oh, now! Just a minute!
ELIZABETH. What is she talking about? Tom!
TOM. About a woman she saw upstairs. But she's made a mistake.
SCOTT. Are you sure, Miss Wellington?
MARTHA. Yes! I'm sure. . . . I'm sorry. I don't mean to—to hurt anybody, but I'm sure.
TOM. (*Grabs* MARTHA *roughly by the arm and swings her around.*) Oh, no! How can you be so sure?
RONNIE. (*Angrily.*) Hey! Let her alone!
TOM. No. I'm going to find out. She's lying or— *How can you be so sure?*
MARTHA. Her shoes! Her shoes! Let me go! I'm not going to answer another question.

(*She breaks away from him and runs through dining area, and out by swinging door.* RONNIE *holds it a second, then goes out after her.*)

TOM. (*To* SCOTT.) That's not an identification!
ELIZABETH. Please! What's this all about?
SCOTT. (*Ignores her; speaks to* TOM.) Maybe not, Mr. Byron—but it's the only one we've got. The only clue we've got. In fact it's the only thing constructive in the whole damned evening. (*To* ELIZABETH.) I hate to tell you this, Miss Byron, but in view of what that girl just said—and in view of your admitting that you—er—blanked out sometimes, I think it likely that you'll be asked to go down to headquarters.
LOUISE. An arrest?
SCOTT. Let's just say for further questioning. I think she ought to be prepared—that's all. Sorry. (*He goes out through Right area, into hall, and to Front Door.*)
ELIZABETH. (*Gives a wry smile.*) I am prepared. That's why I got dressed. Put on these shoes.
TOM. (*Wheels around.*) What's that?
ELIZABETH. You know I don't wear shoes around the house.

Tom. Don't wear—what do you wear?
Elizabeth. What's all this about shoes?
Tom. Never mind! Tell me—what do you wear?
Elizabeth. (*To* Louise.) Slippers. Men never notice anything, do they? I'm on my feet all day. Setting the table—helping the cook—helping to make the beds—
Tom. Then even if you—blacked out—killed Harriet—and then went upstairs, you wouldn't have been wearing shoes, would you?
Elizabeth. Of course not!
Tom. Then the girl is lying! She's lying!
Elizabeth. But why? Why would she lie about me?
Tom. Must be because of Ronnie. Ronnie's in this thing up to his neck. He doped the nurse's ovaltine. It must be— No! No! Maybe she isn't lying. Maybe the woman she saw upstairs *did* have on shoes. But when she saw the others just now they were wearing slippers—or she couldn't see *what* they had on! Their feet were covered up with long negligees—or housecoats—the nurse—Mrs. Smythe—Corinne. You were the only one who had on shoes, so she identified you. But at the time of the murder they *could* have been wearing shoes before they got undressed. Or maybe—maybe— (*He looks over at* Louise.)
Louise. (*Rising.*) Yes, Mr. Byron. *I'm* wearing shoes.
Tom. Yes, you are, aren't you?
Louise. (*Smiles.*) Do you think I was that woman upstairs? Do you think *I* killed Harriet?
Tom. I don't know.
Louise. If I did, you'll have to find a good solid motive. Not anything like—like the reason you had before. Jealousy—to steal a gimmick. That won't wash, I'm afraid.
Tom. No, no! I never really believed that, anyway. (*He suddenly paces towards extreme Left, and starts back.*) Damn! Damn! Damn!
Elizabeth. Tom! What is it?
Tom. A while ago I—I had a flash. An idea about the murder that—that—something somebody said or—or—it

was only a—a—flash, but—something happened that—knocked it right out of my head. Oh! That woman—Mrs. Smythe—came in and screamed. Said I was going to kill her. Oh, yes. I know. The knife! (*Goes towards* LOUISE.) Mrs. Vickers, help me, will you?

LOUISE. I'll do all I can, Mr. Byron.

TOM. You don't want to see my sister arrested for this, do you?

LOUISE. I most certainly do not. I wouldn't like to see anybody arrested for this.

TOM. Harriet was stabbed through the portieres. You wondered why. Why the murderer didn't come into the dining room—and make sure.

LOUISE. Yes. I remember. You said he—or she—the murderer must have called to Harriet—and when she reached the portiere he stabbed her.

TOM. I was wrong. That would have been premeditation. Calling to her. This murder was not premeditated—not by any time at all. I think Harriet heard the murderer just outside—and walked to the doorway to see who it was. Then the murderer struck—struck blindly—four times to make sure. I think the murderer was desperate—in the grip of some over-powering emotion.

ELIZABETH. What emotion, Tom?

TOM. Fear.

ELIZABETH. Fear of what?

TOM. Fear of death.

ELIZABETH. You mean—the murderer thought Harriet was going to kill him?

TOM. Not him. Her! And not fear that Harriet was going to kill her—but fear that she—the murderer—was going to die of a heart attack.

ELIZABETH. But I don't understand. I—

TOM. Please, Liz! Mrs. Vickers—you killed Harriet! She was your heir, wasn't she?

LOUISE. (*After a pause.*) How did you find out?

TOM. I overheard your talk with the policeman—about the nitroglycerin tablets. And I remembered our conversation about Aunt Laura and her will. I said probably none of us would get her two million—she'd leave it to a home for stray cats. You said what a shame it was—that that amount of money—or any amount of money—could do so much good in the hands of the right people. When I asked who were the right people, you said people with pity—understanding—something like that.

LOUISE. You are quite right. I killed Harriet.

ELIZABETH. Oh, no!

LOUISE. After I left Harriet I started for the back stairs. And suddenly—I didn't feel well. I remembered I'd left my bag in the living room, with my heart medicine in it. So I started along the hall there— I must have made some noise—because I heard Harriet coming towards the portieres. By that time I was—well, pretty far gone. I thought I was going to die—die immediately—before I could change my will. Pictures flashed through my mind—like a kaleidoscope! I saw Harriet—harsh—bitter—rude—hating everybody. I leaned against the telephone table—and my hand touched the knife. I had no two million—like your aunt. But I've worked hard—and done well. Eleven books—serial rights—foreign rights—three made into movies. I didn't stop to think what would happen to it all—if Harriet was dead—and I died. I just didn't want her to have it—that's all.

ELIZABETH. Oh, Mrs. Vickers, I—I'm so—

LOUISE. Please! No sympathy. I don't deserve it.

TOM. You went upstairs then?

LOUISE. Yes. I'm not sure how I got there. I suppose I was in a state of shock. (*She smiles.*) I think what shocked me more than anything was that I wasn't dead. I thought I was opening my own door—but it was your aunt's. She saw me with the knife and—well, that part I didn't mean. Truly, I didn't mean any harm to her. The rest—well, you know the rest.

TOM. About the knife?

LOUISE. Yes. I went up to wipe my fingerprints off it. But when I got up there, I—I found I couldn't touch it.

Odd. You can kill someone and be squeamish about blood.

TOM. So you got me to wipe the handle!

ELIZABETH. But how in the world could you carry on, when—

LOUISE. Because all evening I've had the feeling it wasn't really happening—that I was making it up. Of course, I knew I'd be found out—

TOM. And if you hadn't been—

LOUISE. I'd like to think that before I'd let someone else suffer I'd confess.

ELIZABETH. I'm sure you would. (*She takes* LOUISE's *hand.*)

TOM. Is there anything we can do for you?

LOUISE. Yes. Find the lieutenant—tell him what you know—but give me a few minutes alone—to go to my room.

ELIZABETH. (*In alarm.*) You're not going to—I mean, you wouldn't—?

LOUISE. (*She laughs.*) No, I want to write out a new will. As you all know when a person dies intestate—with no family or relative who have a legal claim—the money goes to the state in which he resides. I have nothing against the State of New York—but I can think of some others whom I'd rather benefit. (*Looks at them.*) Please let me go—now—

(ELIZABETH *and* TOM *look at one another, skeptically.*)

TOM. I—I don't know—

LOUISE. You're afraid that I'll kill myself! Oh, no. I could never do that. It may seem strange to you—a murderess—but I believe in God—the only Judge I really have to face that matters. May I go now?

(*They nod sadly. She turns and walks into hall as:*)

THE CURTAIN FALLS

PROPERTY PLOT

ACT ONE:
    Armchair D. R.
    Armchair R.
    Armchair U. C.
    Armchair (low-back) C.
    Armchair D. L.
    Coffee table, before armchair R.
    Dining-room table L.
    5 side chairs (around table) L.
    Built-in sideboard L.
    Telephone table (unseen) in angle of walls C.
    Candlesticks, ornaments, on mantelpiece R.
    Ashtray on coffee table R.
    Telephone on table C.
    Cups, saucers, spoons, on sideboard L.
    Crumpled napkins, dessert plates, forks, on dining table
    Candlesticks, ornaments, on sideboard L.
    Handsome table cover, in drawer of sideboard
    Glasses, on sideboard
    Pitcher of water, on sideboard
    Novel, on dining-room table
    Pint bottle of whiskey, wrapped in table cover, in drawer of sideboard
    Coffee tray, with cups, spoons, sugar bowl, etc. *off* U. C. (MARTHA)
    Cup of coffee, off U. C. (ELIZABETH)
    Notebook, pencil (in Louise's handbag)
    Paper money, in Mrs. Smythe's bag
    Plate, with cheese, crackers, long bread knife *off* U. L. (TOM)
    Phial of tablets, in Louise's handbag
    Bottle of medicine (in Ronnie's pocket)
    2 plates, each with small thermos, cup and saucer, one with crackers on it (*off* U. L. (ELIZABETH)

ACT TWO—*Scene 1*
    Portable typewriter, on dining-room table
    Double sheet yellow paper, no carbon, in typewriter
    Stack of yellow second sheets, beside typewriter
    Piece of white paper, off U. L. (HARRIET)
    Set of portieres, on pole, *off* U. C. (TOM)
    Spoon (in Martha's apron pocket)

ACT Two—*Scene 2*
   Shawl—*off* U. C. (TOM)
   Cigarette lighter *off* U. C. (LOUISE)
   Garden shears (on telephone table)

ACT THREE:
   Yellow paper (in Louise's handbag)

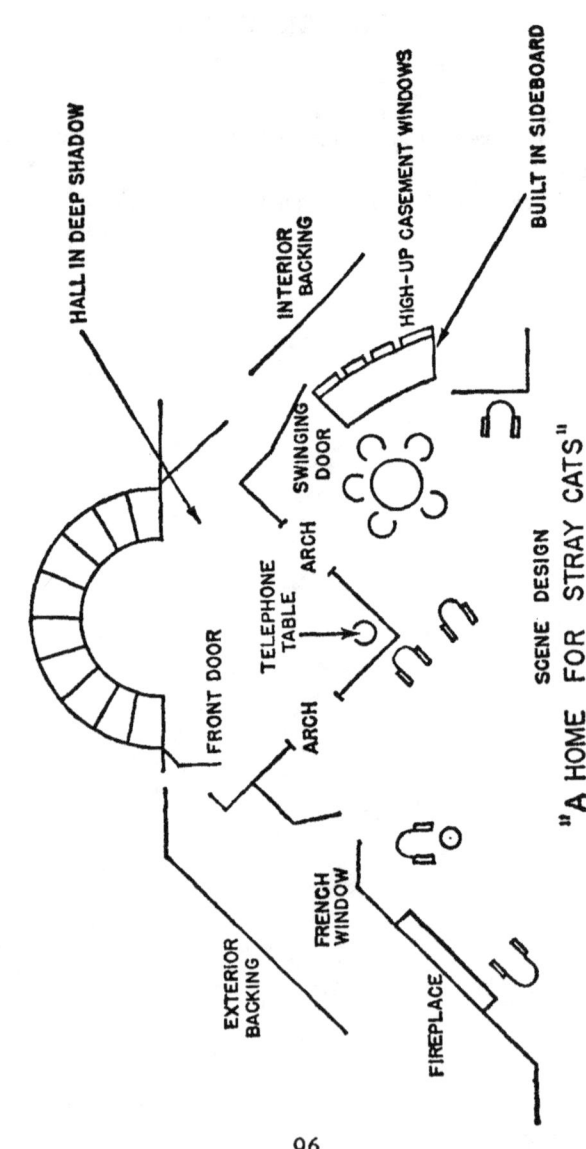

MUSIC USE NOTE

Licensees are solely responsible for obtaining formal written permission from copyright owners to use copyrighted music in the performance of this play and are strongly cautioned to do so. If no such permission is obtained by the licensee, then the licensee must use only original music that the licensee owns and controls. Licensees are solely responsible and liable for all music clearances and shall indemnify the copyright owners of the play(s) and their licensing agent, Samuel French, against any costs, expenses, losses and liabilities arising from the use of music by licensees. Please contact the appropriate music licensing authority in your territory for the rights to any incidental music.

IMPORTANT BILLING AND CREDIT REQUIREMENTS

If you have obtained performance rights to this title, please refer to your licensing agreement for important billing and credit requirements.

www.ingramcontent.com/pod-product-compliance
Lightning Source LLC
Chambersburg PA
CBHW051407290426
44108CB00015B/2190